I Pray Hardest When I'm Being Shot At

KYLE GARRET

D1737208

HELLGATE PRESS   ASHLAND, OREGON

I Pray Hardest When I'm Being Shot At
©2011 KYLE GARRET

Published by Hellgate Press
(An imprint of L&R Publishing, LLC)

All rights reserved. No part of this publication may be reproduced or used in any form or by any means, graphic, electronic or mechanical, including photocopying, recording, taping, or information and retrieval systems without written permission of the publisher.

Hellgate Press
PO Box 3531
Ashland, OR 97520
www.hellgatepress.com

Editing: Harley B. Patrick
Cover design: L. Redding
Cover photo: Robert Stuart, Australia, 1944

Library of Congress Cataloging-in-Publication Data is available upon request.

ISBN: 978-1-55571-6868

Printed and bound in the United States of America
First edition 10 9 8 7 6 5 4 3 2

For Papa

Contents

PART ONE: LOVE & WAR

PART TWO: HOW DID I GET HERE?

PART THREE: ELLIPSIS

PART ONE

Love & War

1

"Don't You Know There's a War On?"

THIS IS A BOOK ABOUT LOVE AND WAR.

My grandparents had a love affair of over sixty years. Three generations of my family have served in the military, spanning Pancho Villa's attack on U.S. soil to Vietnam. In my family, love and war were nearly inseparable.

This book is about two people who reconnected through chance, through the most impractical and romantic of ways, who took a lot of chances, and who tried to give up, but couldn't. It's about a man and a woman who lived through some of the most significant times in American history, yet always cared most about each other and the family they would bring into this world. This is a book about love and war, but it's also about two singular people who played very small roles in a grand play, and who were just looking to find some happiness during turbulent times.

This is the story of my grandparents, one a three war veteran and retired major, the other an unsung, forerunner of a new generation of women. It's the story of two extremes, love and war, and how it changed their lives, and how writing about their lives, in turn, changed mine.

"Your grandfather doesn't talk about it much," says my mom. I called her because I needed some background information on Papa's military career. She tells me she has letters that Papa sent his sister while he was in basic training and that she'll mail them to me.

My grandfather doesn't talk about any of the wars he's fought in and, according to my mom, he thinks that books about war are written by people who've never experienced them. Perhaps that's just the stoicism of his generation, or perhaps it's an internalization that can only come from experiencing war. Either way, it makes the path ahead of me fairly daunting.

"That makes it very hard to write a book about him," I say.

My grandfather and I don't have a lot in common, at least not on paper. He was born on February 17, 1924. I was born on October 3, 1975. He grew up in Warren, Ohio, the same town as my grandmother. I live in Los Angeles and my girlfriend has never set foot in the Buckeye state. My grandfather is a Lutheran and a Republican. I'm an agnostic and a Democrat. He's short and rather stocky. I'm tall and incredibly thin. He subscribes to Omaha steaks. I'm a vegetarian. And, perhaps most importantly at this point, he's a retired major and three war veteran. I've never even fired a gun.

Prior to the start of my research, my grandfather had only ever offered two anecdotes on his time at war. The first was an offhand, almost random comment he made to my dad, mentioning that South Vietnamese pilots always flew above the U.S. helicopters, even after being specifically told to fly below them. This meant the U.S. pilots, whose number included my grandfather, had to watch out for fire from both below and above.

I can't imagine placing yourself in a position where you will not only lose your life, but more than likely do so in an extremely unpleasant way. Maybe your body will be recovered, maybe it won't. And those people back home who love you will find out about it days later. Thousands of miles away and days later, they'll get a knock on the door or a phone call telling them that you're dead and that there was nothing they could do about it.

I imagine that's the hardest part: the feeling of helplessness.

Every day could be your last and my grandfather had entire years worth of those days. From high above the South Pacific, to the DMZ in Korea and the jungles of Vietnam, he continually put his life at risk, yet somehow he always came back.

"The best thing to do would be to go over there with a bottle of whiskey and just get him talking," says my mom, still on the phone.

She's right; that would be the best thing to do. Unfortunately, I live in Los Angeles, California and Papa currently resides in Huber Heights, Ohio. I won't see him again until sometime in July and I don't want to wait that long.

I've sent him e-mails for some basic information, like where he was stationed and when. I ask him what operations he went on. At this point I just want the bare bones. I know I'll need more and I suppose the most logical solution would be to call him, but the more I think about it the less helpful I think that would actually be. My grandfather has always kept to himself about pretty much everything, something I'm just now picking up on.

I don't see him opening up on the phone.

There are some nights that I lie in bed and think of all the friends my grandfather must have lost, all the people he saw die—all the people he had to kill just to survive. And I know that even when I start to get a few more pieces of this puzzle, that I won't be able to do justice to the scope and scale of war. I have no way to measure it. War is a language I don't speak and there is no translator.

Thankfully, while my grandfather might be hesitant to talk about his life, both in wartime and in peace, my grandmother has no such reservations.

During the summer of 2003 I sent my grandfather a tape recorder and a package of audio tapes. It was my hope that he would use these to record his history, that perhaps an oral retelling would be easier and faster for him than a written one. But he would never use the machine or the tapes.

My grandmother, on the other hand, sent me two audio tapes that she'd filled with her memoirs. She'd already hand written and then typed them, so it was just a simple matter for her to sit down and read them aloud.

Being the technophile that I am, I actually had no way to listen to them. It wouldn't have been hard for me to find a way—a Walkman would be pretty cheap—but I let them sit on a shelf in my closet as I busied myself with another book, one that was more indicative of my life at that moment.

It took me two and a half years to get to those tapes.

By that time, my girlfriend Nicole and I had moved in together and she happened to actually own a Walkman. This began a string of days that involved me with headphones on, listening to my grandmother's tapes, and taking fairly extensive notes.

And by "fairly extensive" I mean pages upon pages, because my grand-mother has a memory like an elephant. She can tell you what she had for dinner on the first night of the train ride she took from Warren, Ohio to El Centro California in June of 1945 (it was chicken). She can even tell you how much it cost (they bought a full meal for a dollar). And what song was popular on the radio ("Sentimental Journey").

My grandmother, Elizabeth Anne Davis, was born on May 3rd, 1926 in Lynchburg, Ohio to Griffith John Davis and Alta Elizabeth Green Davis. She was delivered by Dr. Tyler, who made a house call. She was the youngest of four children: her brothers Sheldon and Ned and her sister Eleanor.

Grandma's mom would die just six days shy of her daughter's eighteenth birthday. She'd had an enlarged thyroid for years, a condition which her father—my great-great-grandfather—had also had. He died during surgery to treat the problem, which made my grandmother's mom apprehensive about having it dealt with. That apprehension ultimately cost her much needed time and she would die before she even turned fifty.

Losing her mom at such a young age would be really hard for my grandmother, and as years went by that void in her life would show up at major crossroads, determining how she would choose to live her life. It would affect how her relationship with Papa played out, I think, as well as her relationship with her own daughter.

Griffith, grandma's father, would later remarry. His choice of second wife came as a bit of a surprise to me.

"Good god," I said aloud, even though no one was in the room with me.

I hit the "stop" button on the Walkman and took off my headphones. Nicole was in the shower, but I was so stunned by what I'd just heard I needed to tell her right away.

"Hey," I yelled from outside the bathroom. I didn't want to startle her. I'd done that before and she had the razor blade gash on her leg to prove it.

"Hey," she said.

"So get this," I said as I cracked the door open a bit so she could hear me better, "my grandma's father married his brother-in-law's widow."

"What?"

"That's what *I* said. Evidently my grandma's mom's brother Clarence had been gassed in World War I and left behind a widow named Eleanor —my grandma's aunt through marriage."

"Right," said Nicole.

"So a year and a half after his first wife died, my grandmother's dad married her aunt Eleanor."

"That's bizarre."

"Seriously. I have enough trouble trying to change the image Ohioans have. This isn't going to help things."

To be clear, the marriage actually made sense and wasn't really that creepy. Eleanor and Griffith weren't related by blood. In fact, I would imagine they had a lot in common, being part of the same family. They'd probably known each other for a long time.

But there's still something kind of strange about it.

"You're really jumping into this," said Nicole. This was perhaps the fourth time I'd interrupted her shower with some new insight into my family history.

"I know," I said as I headed back out to the living, back to the Walkman and the tapes. "It's weird."

He Said—She Said

> He: *We met in the West side park when you were ten and I was twelve.*
> She: *I don't remember.*
> She: *You sat behind me at a football game when I was a sophomore and you were a senior. You asked me out after the game.*
> He: *I don't remember*

This is the response I got from my grandparents when I asked them how they met. While I was initially frustrated that they didn't just send me a quick e-mail with the information, the letter I got was well worth the wait.

I love the fact that my grandfather remembers when they first met, yet has no recollection of asking her out that first time. Papa's memory seems to be strangely more romantic, while grandma's is more practical, which, really, is a great way to describe my grandparents' relationship.

My grandmother first mentions my grandfather in her memoirs in a chapter she calls "Don't You Know There's a War On?" She mentions that both of her older brothers were drafted when the U.S. entered WWII, although one didn't go to Europe until the post-war occupation and the other was blind in one eye, so he was never sent overseas. For her part, my grandmother decided to join other high school girls in writing letters to soldiers in Europe and the South Pacific. Grandma saw a familiar name of the list of soldiers to choose from: Robert M. Stuart.

The decision on whether or not to enlist was not an easy one for my grandfather. At the time, the draft stopped at twenty-one, which meant that if he were going to serve, he would have to do so voluntarily. And while he came from a military background, he found a good job at the local Copperweld steel mill as soon as he graduated from high school. He was even making enough money to take flying lessons, which was a dream come true.

But the call of duty was too strong for Papa to ignore for very long. He enlisted that fall, beginning basic training in September of 1942. My grandma began sending him letters in the spring of '43, when he was stationed in Florida for radar and gunnery training.

"At school, names of service men who would like to receive mail were available," wrote my grandma. "Since I had dated Robert M. Stuart when he was a senior and I was a sophomore, I began a correspondence with him. He was a gunner on a B-17 in the Marines. He caught me by surprise with so much interest. His Mother called me and invited me over and sent me flowers as often as Stu directed."

Papa's interest was so great that he spent his last night stateside not with his family, but with my grandmother. He went with her to the Friendship Club formal dance towards the end of December of 1943, just before he shipped out to the South Pacific.

At this point, however, I get the distinct impression that they're relationship wasn't really that serious and probably seemed more important to my grandfather than to my grandmother. And if it were important to him at this point, I could only imagine how much more valuable it would be while spending his nights flying over the Japanese occupied islands.

Grandma's only comment regarding Papa before he left for the South Pacific was that they'd dated when she was a sophomore. Honestly, I didn't know people did such things in the '40s. I thought it was sock hop, malt shop, Enchantment Under Sea, marriage. I didn't know it was possible to date someone and then stop dating them.

Then again, my grandparents would end up getting married twice; it's clear there's nothing ordinary about them.

It's occurred to me, as I try to piece together the story of my grandfather's life, that the frame of this house is going to end up being built by my grandmother. Papa didn't seem to fully understand the magnitude of the life he was leading, but I think my grandmother did. I think it's part of the reason their marriage was so successful, the fact that they viewed the world in differing, yet complimentary, ways.

But my grandmother doesn't know a lot of the details of Papa's military career aside from locations and dates. I have a letter from my grandfather chronicling his military career as far as where he was stationed, what he was training for, and what types of aircraft he flew, but I have little to no detail on the specifics of any of that. I know only the vaguest bits about what kinds of missions he was on, from bombing depots to maintaining supply lines, to search and destroy. Every single day that he was on duty there was the opportunity for any level of combat and I really don't know about any of it—but I've only just begun digging.

I can tell you where my grandparents were living on any given date of the past sixty years. I can tell you what rank my grandfather had attained by that point. I can tell you what kind of house they had and how much money they made. But I don't know how Papa felt. I don't know what it was like to fear for your life on a regular basis for days, weeks, months at a time.

I think, perhaps, the best way to start is to figure out why he decided to enlist.

2

Beginnings

It got cold at night in Columbus, New Mexico. When the sun went down, the temperature would drop a good twenty degrees, and the small town just a few miles from the Mexico/United States border felt like it could have been anywhere in the Midwest. This probably gave Seth Robert Stuart some comfort. It was a little taste of his home, minus the snow that would invariably be falling this time of year back east.

Seth was asleep at two in the morning on March 9, 1916, as were most of the U.S. 13th Cavalry. They were all awoken the same way, by a clear, distinctive call to arms: gunfire.

Pancho Villa, the famed Mexican revolutionary, had launched an attack on American soil.

In September of 2004, my grandfather—Seth's son—sent me a manila envelope. This was a little surprising because, up until this point, my grandfather as been pretty slow as far as giving me material for the book. The envelope, however, wasn't about Papa; it was about his father.

Seth, who went by S. Robert Stuart, enlisted in the U.S. cavalry in 1912 at the age of twenty. He trained at a small facility in Columbus, Ohio and was later assigned to the 13th Cavalry, who were primarily assigned to patrol the U.S./Mexico border which included Columbus, New Mexico. At the time, though, the U.S. had a good relationship with Pancho Villa, and an attack on U.S. soil was unlikely.

The manila envelope contained pictures of my great grandfather: one by himself, one with his troop, and one with his horse "Rags." It came with a letter from my grandfather explaining what everything was, including two photocopied newspaper articles. One was written by my great grand-father for a regional newspaper in Warren, Ohio. It chronicled the battle at Columbus, New Mexico.

The second article was written by Papa, and appeared in a southwest regional magazine in the '50s. It also retold that battle at Columbus, al-though I think hindsight and research afforded my grandfather a little bit more detail in his version. He did say, however, that he wrote the article "for the magnificent sum of thirty bucks which made me decide to stay in the Army and not try to make a living as a writer."

To this day, historians disagree on why, exactly, Villa decided to invade the small town of Columbus, New Mexico. Ultimately, his motives didn't matter. All that mattered was that his forces outnumbered the American soldiers by two-to-one, as most accounts put the number of U.S. soldiers between 250-350, and the number of soldiers in Villa's force as 500-700. They had numbers, preparation, and the element of surprise on their side. But the U.S. had better weapons, dedicated soldiers, and a little bit of luck on theirs.

While the majority of the 13th Cavalry might have been asleep when Villa launched his attack, they knew better than to let their guard down.

"When they broke out of the ditch they were immediately discovered by the sentry on No. 3 post," wrote my great grandfather, "who gave the alarm as only a horse soldier knows how, by opening fire. When he was found his rifle was empty and three rounds fired from his pistol. Today he would have been cited for a Congressional Medal of Honor. Then it was considered all in a day's work."

Villa had also underestimated the cavalry's ability to react quickly. They were up and armed in a matter of moments, "the most undressed army that ever fought a battle," said my great grandfather.

To make matters worse for Villa's troops, they had decided to set a three story hotel on fire. The blaze lit up the entire town, not only giving the U.S. soldiers light to aim by, but providing the smaller force shadows to use for cover. While the goal might have been the complete destruction of Columbus, New Mexico, Villa had only succeeded in leveling the battlefield and he was soon sounding the alarm to retreat.

My great grandfather added this bit to his story, a funny anecdote that's perhaps only truly funny to someone who had been through such a fight. One of the lieutenants had been wounded and had to drop to the back of the patrol. He picked out a target—a Mexican revolutionary on a big, white mule—and commanded three soldiers to "get the SOB on the white mule." My great grandfather was one of those three soldiers. The man fell off the mule after they'd fired ten or eleven rounds. The lieutenant then yelled at the cavalrymen for taking so many rounds to knock him off, since two of them were expert riflemen and one was a sharpshooter.

Seth would eventually switch from cavalry to field artillery, just so he could go to France to fight in WWI. He would leave the military in 1920, after meeting my great grandmother. As my grandfather said in the letter to me, "... Army pay, for the most part, was insufficient to marry (so) he left..."

I never met my great grandfather and I don't know the type of relationship he had with Papa. I don't know that he ever put any kind of pressure on his son to enlist, either before or after Pearl Harbor. But I'm sure Seth's example must have made an impression on his son. While Seth spent his career leading and riding horses, Papa would take to the skies, first in planes, then in helicopters. And while Seth's time in the military lasted only eight years, Papa would make a life for himself in the armed services.

My grandfather's only son, my uncle Rob, spent a short time in the navy, perhaps completing some sort of military trinity of by land, by sea, and by air. His was a brief and tumultuous stay, however, and it was clear that the military, for him, was just one more attempt at finding his place. My brother and I really never showed any interest in serving our country and would be the generation to end our family's line of military service. I have to admit that I feel a little bad about that, as if I've failed to keep my family's legacy alive.

My great grandfather died of a heart attack on November 9, 1952, nearly twenty-three years before I'd be born. He passed on a desire to serve his country and a desire to write. It's nice to think that at least some part of him managed to make the long journey to his great grandson.

If my grandfather was persuaded to enlist in the U.S. military by anything other than a sense of patriotism, it might have been an opportunity to fly. It's not something I've ever really considered before, Papa's love of flying. I had seen the old pictures of him in the fashionable pilot's jackets. I knew that his hearing wasn't very good because of years spent near jet engines. And every single time I flew home for any reason, my grandfather would ask me what kind of plane I'd been on. But I never thought of Papa as a pilot and I'm not sure why. I think, perhaps, it was because when I finally knew him, he was too old to pilot a plane or a helicopter, and, during my lifetime, would soon be too old to even make it as a passenger.

Papa's first opportunity to fly came from his Uncle Frank Dewberry, who lived in New Castle, Pennsylvania. Uncle Frank bought a Piper Cub twin engine plane so his three boys could learn to fly and managed to introduce the flying bug to his nephew in Ohio. "Uncle Frank, by the way," wrote Papa in another letter he sent me, "was the 'better off' relative, winter home in Florida, etc."

Fortunately for Papa, he had an option closer to home for flying. The father of his friend "Chubby" Lyons had been an Air Force pilot until the

Great Depression, when he'd been let go to cut costs. "He owned and operated the Warren, Ohio airport and gave flying lessons there," wrote Papa. "Grass strip, hangars, etc."

Papa flew as often as he could afford to, which, after graduating and getting a job at the Copperweld Steel Company, was pretty often. But his sense of duty nagged at him, preventing him from truly enjoying his first summer as an adult.

"As the war really cranked up, I was torn to 'go' as opposed to making good bucks at Copperweld and flying when I could afford it. In those days the 'draft' only went down to twenty-one years old.

"By fall, I couldn't put it off any longer. Late September I enlisted in the Marine Corps…"

Papa's decision came with a little fanfare, courtesy of the local paper: "Robert Stuart, 18, son of Mr. and Mrs. Robert Stuart, 1835 Front SW, has enlisted in the Marine Corps and gone to Parris Island, South Carolina, for training. He was graduated in the June 1942 class at Harding High School."

This wouldn't be my grandfather's first appearance in the local paper, both because of his achievements and because of a love of writing letters. Before my grandmother ever entered the picture, my grandfather was already maintaining correspondence with a number of people; he decided to add the *Warren Tribune Chronicle* to that list.

Papa's letter was a rebuttal to a previous letter regarding the draft, written by someone known only as "Fifteen." It's entitled "A Marine's View":

I'm a Marine in training at Parris [sic] Island, S.C. I was just reading in "Everybody's Say-So" "Fifteen's" view of the 18-19 draft (Sat., Oct. 31). I'm now 18, soon will be 19, and I hope to be in action before I'm 20.

She speaks of an over-age man without draft age children advocating

18-19 draft. I believe she was rather impolite but I'm an 18-year-old already in the service giving my views.

One of the first sensations I can remember was of being very proud of my father for being an overseas veteran of the last war. That is only a soldier's due. I come from a fighting family. When duty called, they never failed to answer. That may be a bit off the subject but it forms the background.

A noted militarist once said, "A war must be fought in two ways, the caution of older men and the courage of youth."

The Marine Corps of today is made up of a great many 18, 19, and 20 year olds. Look what those "kids" did in the Solomons!

Papa's referring to the Battle of Guadalcanal in August of '42, which saw the U.S. and Allied Forces engaged in intense fighting with the Japanese. The Marines landed on Guadalcanal and managed to hold out under constant Japanese attack for months. This gave the U.S. a foothold in the South Pacific, allowing them to launch their campaign against the Japanese.

Papa's letter in the newspaper continues:

It's the blind courage that overwhelms odds and wins battles. I don't expect to come back. If, in the line of duty, I must die, then I shall. I'm proud to fight for my country! That may seem brutal. Of course, parents hate to see their young sons going into the horrors of war. That's only natural; but if the President and the Army heads feel that to win the war they need the younger men, then they should be proud to go. This is war. We're not playing any more. It's either life or death for us or the enemy. Regardless of issues or views, it's our duty to win. Petty feelings must be put aside. This is not time for weak-kneed interference. I think "Fifteen" should go back to her school books and leave fighting to those who aren't afraid. I think the lowest form of man are those fellows of 18 and 19 who are afraid of the draft.

Some may call me a fanatic. I'm not really. I'm just saying what millions of my "buddies" think.

I'll admit I was a little shocked by the intensity of the letter. In fact, I had some reservations about even including it. This is not the Papa I know and I'm not sure that I want this side of him to be seen so early on in this book.

But I have to remember that he was only eighteen then and, even more importantly, that he'd yet to go to war. I would imagine you have to adopt a certain mentality when preparing for war. You can't allow yourself to let fear creep in and Papa, in all of his eighteen years, had taken that philosophy to the extreme, going so far as to blacklist anyone his age that wasn't eager to be drafted. Papa of sixty-four years later might still hold the same beliefs, but they've been tempered by time and experience.

During basic training at Parris Island, South Carolina, Papa went through the usual routine of tests that determine IQ, fitness, aptitudes, etc. The fact that he was in good shape, had perfect vision, and knew how to fly made Papa a perfect candidate for Marine Corps Aviation. He was then sent to Cherry Point, North Carolina for even more tests, these to determine exactly which aspect of aviation he'd be assigned.

After that, he was sent to Florida, first for radio/radar school at Cecil Field Naval Air Station in Jacksonville, then to aerial gunnery school in Hollywood, just north of Miami.

"Radio school was actually operated the same as radio for ship board use," wrote Papa. "More code, key operation, sending and receiving, etc. The only difference we did not get typewriter training. Shipboard operators typed incoming 'traffic.' Aviators took it by hand and printing, as I have done ever since. With incoming at about forty words a minute that's fast printing!"

Radar was a huge part of the U.S. success in World War II, allowing U.S. ships and planes to spot enemy forces hundreds of miles away. It made the bombing runs in the South Pacific all the more effective.

"At the time, radar was highly classified," wrote Papa, "so the school was in a separate building, fenced, barbed wire topped. Guard at the door check to see you had been 'cleared' to go there, etc. Classes covered theory of radar, setting up equipment, interpreting incoming images, and a lot more stuff I have long forgotten."

Gunnery training in Hollywood was much different. Papa said they did skeet shooting to practice. The airborne training would happen in Jacksonville, where they would perform actual aerial firing drills from operational PBY's. PBY's were naval flying boats that were used in the 30s and 40s. The PB stood for Patrol Bomber and the Y was the manufacturers' identification. The planes could be equipped with depth chargers, bombs, torpedoes, or .50 caliber machine guns.

"Targets were towed by an aircraft pulling long white canvas targets," wrote Papa. "Each student had a can of ammo rolls with the nose of each round painted a different color. After a day's training these targets were examined back at Cecil to evaluate each student's performance. Each hole in the target would show the color of the bullet that had hit it. Neat, huh?"

But their duties didn't just consist of training. Cecil Field was an active Naval base, so while part of the day was spent training, the rest of the time was spent patrolling the shipping routes off the Florida coast for German submarines. "At the time, subs had to surface every so often to charge their batteries, change air for crew, etc. If a PBY could catch a sub on the surface it had hundred pound bombs in racks under each wing to drop on it."

While they never spotted a sub, they had some run-ins with a few unfortunate whales, which looked like submarines when they were coming for air. Fortunately, the pilots realized they weren't Germans before they launched an attack. Still, being on high alert and having to suddenly call off an attack must have been excellent training in preparation for the real thing. It also makes me wonder how many whales must have died during World War II.

Papa finally graduated in the middle of 1943 and was sent back to Cherry Point, before moving on to Peter Field Point near Jacksonville,

North Carolina. He would spend the rest of the year in advanced training, preparing for his eventual assignment to the South Pacific.

"Oh, hey, let me check the mail," I said as Nicole and I waited for the elevator up to our apartment. We'd just gotten home from dinner with some friends. We'd spent the day inside cleaning, so neither of us had gotten around to checking the mail.

I found the usual assortment of bills and credit card offers, but I also found a small, manila envelope from my mom.

We got into the elevator as I started opening the envelope. It was pretty tightly packed. My parents would occasionally send me newspaper clippings they thought I'd find interesting or letters from my alma mater that still went to my last known permanent address. But this envelope seemed far too full for that.

As we got off the elevator I pulled a stack of letters out of the envelope.

"Oh, these are those letters Papa wrote to his sister!"

When we got into our apartment we both began looking them over. There were eleven letters in all, running from April to December of 1943, as well as a note from my mom saying that they led up to my grandfather's deployment to the South Pacific.

"Look at the date on the postal stamp," I said, "1943!"

"Smell them," said Nicole as she moved one away from her nose and held it up to mine. They smelled old, like secret, ancient tomes known only to a few.

There were also four pictures: my great grandfather (looking dapper in a suit and hat), my great grandmother (a portrait shot from the '60s), a second picture of my great grandmother (this from 1943, coincidentally the same year my grandfather wrote these letters), and a group shot of my great grandfather, great grandmother, her sister, my grandfather, his sister, and a neighbor. I actually mistook the picture of my great grandfather for my grandfather at first, the similarities were that striking.

This was it. This was what I was looking for. I was finally going to get a personal glimpse at what my grandfather's life was like during this pivotal time in his life.

This book was finally coming together.

Almost everything I know about my grandfather's sister, Betty, comes from the letters he wrote her when he was in basic training. My grandmother actually only mentions her three times in her memoirs. The first time is to mention that her prenatal doctor was Betty's boss, as Betty was a nurse. The second is that Betty helped give her mom support when Seth Stuart died. And the final mention is of her death, although my grandparents didn't go to her funeral.

I e-mailed my mom about this and she told me that she remembers her aunt being a "prickly pear." I realize that the sister-in-law is probably not a big part in the story of anyone's life, but it still seems odd that grandma only mentioned her three times. Even stranger is the fact that, given the stack of letters I now had, Papa seemed somewhat close to her, at least when he was younger.

But I don't have a sister, so I have no idea what that relationship might be like.

It's easy to imagine that Betty was just protective of her brother. Given the extremes of grandma and Papa's time together—particularly the first few years—it's easy to imagine that only my grandparents truly understood what their relationship was all about. From the outside, however, it might not have seemed very healthy.

The last letter is dated December 13, 1943, just ten days before Papa would head back to Warren, Ohio for his last leave of absence before heading off to the South Pacific. As I mentioned earlier, he would spend his last night stateside with my grandmother at the Friendship Club formal dance instead of spending it with his family, which could have marked the beginning of tension between grandma and her future sister-in-law.

My grandfather calls his sister "chum" a lot. And he signs his letters "Bob," a name I don't associate with him, even if his given name is Robert. My grandmother has always called him "Stu."

It's funny to read these letters having the knowledge that I do. In the first letter he talks about marriage: "Of course a wife has to be a guy's pal, too. I know if I ever marry, I'll want my wife to be a girl I can consider my best pal as well as the woman I love."

My grandfather's view on long distance relationships seems well laid out, too: "You know, you mentioned in your letter the fact that you wonder what I'm going to do about the girls I pal around with at different bases. Well, I'll tell you, there's no sense in writing, that only prolongs things. I think the best thing to do is just break things off completely when you leave. Perhaps it's a little brutal, but it's really the only solution."

I wonder if Betty ever showed these letters to Papa years later. Her son gave them to my mom, who probably assumed that my grandmother had seen them, even though she hadn't. I'm sure grandma would find it interesting that the man who so intently pursued her through letters thought that long distance relationships were a bad idea. Clearly, it just took the right girl to change his mind.

Girls were, of course, very much on Papa's mind. He was in the Marines, after all. He was going to serve his country. Patriotism in 1943 was one heck of an aphrodisiac.

For example: "Believe it or not, but I'm a new man if you know what I mean. For the past month I have lived like an angel. I think it must be the heat. Mostly I guess because I've been getting fed up with the crowd I've been running with. That, however, is, personal problems."

I'm not sure what "a new man" means entirely, but I get the impression that the "old man" was in direct opposition to living "like an angel." This was in a letter dated September 16, 1943. By that time, he would have been exchanging letters with my grandmother on a regular basis. My grandfather was apparently getting more serious about that particular correspondence, to the point of changing his lifestyle.

To continue with a trend: "Pat wrote a very nice letter, she asked me to come and visit her and Ward if I should get home. She naturally didn't mention the reason for her quick marriage. As she put it, she just 'decided' to get married. Ah, this strange world!"

I have no idea who Pat or Ward are, but this letter would end up being prophetic. While my grandmother would get pregnant not long after they got married, their daughter, my mom, would follow Pat and Ward's route. Perhaps Papa should have passed this story on to his daughter. Then again, I suppose it's good that he didn't, or I might not be here right now, as my parents never would have gotten married.

As for downtime between training: "Went out on a bit of a tear last night, the first real outing I've had since I came back. Kentucky bourbon straight all night and without any chasers either. A wonderful time was had by all." Living "like an angel," might have steered Papa away from the ladies, but he was still a young man out to enjoy himself.

Funny enough, my first thought upon reading about Papa's night out drinking, aside from the fact that I'm a Tennessee whiskey drinker myself, is that, for as long as I've known him, my grandfather has always drank Canadian whiskey. Now I'm wondering if perhaps that's the real story here: the evolution of a man and his drink of choice.

There's actually one letter written on the radio log sheet of a plane Papa was flying on one day. "If this letter is a bit jerky it's because it's extremely rough up here today."

Papa mentions in one of his letters that he's received notes from a number of people and that keeping up on his correspondences was somewhat taxing and often times boring. But he does it nonetheless, because he knows he won't get new letters unless he answers the old ones.

The strange thing about the letters is the summer camp quality to them. Here he is, preparing to be sent to the South Pacific to fight the Japanese during World War II and my grandfather is writing about girls, drinking, and family gossip. The simple fact that he had the time and energy to write at all while undergoing Marine Corps training is astounding.

And as frustrating as it might be to wait for letters from my grandfather that answer questions that I've e-mailed to him, I suppose there's a certain symmetry to it, a certain appropriateness to it, as if this book couldn't be written in any other way.

3

World War II

ALL PAPA COULD DO WAS GRIT his teeth and hold on. All he could do was hope that his pilot, Ray Smith, had enough skill to make up for his bad luck, because they were hundreds of miles away from the air strip and they were down to one, barely functioning engine. They were in the skies above the Bismarck Archipelago, machine guns and anti-aircraft guns blazing away at them, just praying they could make it back without going down.

And that was just one of their thirty-five combat missions.

Just after Christmas, 1943, Papa was recalled early as his unit was moving to Marine Corps Air Station El Centro, CA. Papa had been assigned to a PBJ, the Navy designation for the Air Corps B-25, which was a medium bomber. He was part of the VMB 433 squadron, which stood for "heavier than air Marine bomber" (V meaning heavier than air, as opposed to L which meant lighter than air and signified balloons and the like). The squadron was known as the "Forked Tailed Devils."

Papa was assigned to a flight crew made up of pilot Ray Smith, co-pilot Hugh Price, a navigator named Young ("later a fellow named Henry," although Papa never says what happened to Young), turret gunner Don Keefe, tail gunner David Cosby, and Papa, the radio/waist gunner.

"Each (PBJ) had two full crews assigned to it and moves like that the pilots flipped coins to see which crew got to fly the 'bird' and which one had to go with ground people by rail," Papa said about the trip to El Centro. "Our pilot was a lousy gambler, we went to El Centro by rail, the other crew flew out."

Unfortunately for Papa, his pilot's bad luck continued, so he and his crew had to take a boat from San Diego. "The ship was the 'HMS Brastogi,' a Dutch freighter that had been in the Indonesian commercial business. When the Japanese were overrunning all the Pacific islands, the captain and crew sailed to our west coast and re-fitted as a troop carrier under contract to the U.S. Only memorable thing about it was we were the first ship leaving San Diego for the Pacific alone, not in a convoy."

The trip took thirty days, but Papa and his crew finally arrived in the New Hebrides Group, a collection of islands in the South Pacific now known as Vanuatu. From there they flew north to Guadalcanal's Henderson Field, as the Marines had taken control of Guadalcanal from the Japanese the year before. They again went north to a "dot" in the ocean called Green Island, a place I'm having absolutely no luck finding on a map. There Papa's crew was operational for a few weeks, bombing various Japanese held positions. But they moved again rather quickly, this time past Japanese held New Ireland to Emirau Island, which is currently a part of New Ireland and a province of Papua New Guinea. Papa was stationed as close to a Japanese held island as possible.

I do my best to search the internet to find all of these locations. I pull maps of every cluster of islands in the South Pacific. Some are easy to find, like Guadalcanal. Some, like Green Island, are just impossible to find. Through a series of trial and error (and numerous spellings), I finally find Emirau Island, which is obviously the most important one.

I'm finally able to find a map that has both New Ireland and Emirau Island on it. And there's a key. It shows distance in kilometers, so I do my best estimation from the map and then head off in search of a metric converter.

In my head I'm picturing my grandfather, all of twenty years old, stationed at this small base on Emirau Island, away from his family and his friends, and less than thirty miles away from the enemy.

It's March 30th and my mom called today to tell me that yesterday my grandfather was taken to the emergency room.

According to my mom, he's fine now. She said he might even go home tomorrow. She said he had fluid in his lungs and between medications and a blood transfusion (something about iron), they were able to fix it. She made it seem like it was situation normal.

Acting like everything's fine when everything isn't is something of an art form in my family. We don't like to worry people and we never ask for help. So imagine something serious first being filtered through my grandmother (who no doubt called my mom) and then being filtered through my mom. I'm getting watered down news. I'm only getting one version of events: the one everyone considers easiest to deal with.

There's really no way for me to gauge the seriousness of the situation with any kind of certainty, but that doesn't stop me from becoming a bit freaked out by the timing.

Writing this book scares me. There's really only one definitive ending to the story of someone's life and there's a part of me deep down that honestly believes I've set things into motion by writing this book.

Fortunately, there's also a part of me who sees these events more as wake up calls than as life imitating art, or at least taking notes from it. There's a part of me who sees this as a very big, flashing neon sign that says "Get off your ass and write while you have time."

I've wasted so much time for so long. I've put this off forever. And now I feel like I'm fighting some clock.

Because tonight my grandfather is lying in a military hospital in Ohio and he's eighty-two and in this book he's on Emirau Island and he's only twenty.

I have sixty-two years to cover and I don't know how much time I have left.

My grandfather took part in routine bombing of the Japanese occupied islands in the South Pacific. Most of their targets were supply depots and the like, all done in an effort to keep the Japanese on their guard. Unfortunately, the best way to surprise them was to fly in at night and, ideally, during rainstorms, because Japanese anti-aircraft batteries used sound and sight (search lights) to aim. So Papa would sit in the radio operator's compartment in his B-25 as they flew over enemy territory at night, in rainstorms. The armor in Papa's section of the plane was only a half an inch thick, and even that was as thick as it got throughout the plane. A half an inch of metal was the only thing keeping them safe.

"Concept was simple," Papa wrote. "With our radar, identify the entry point, take up the specified compass heading, time to target, drop all or part of that load of ordinance, and come home. Simple but a little hairy."

On top of that, these were supposed to be surprise attacks, which meant it was a single aircraft mission. The idea wasn't to begin an invasion, it was to keep the Japanese confused and on alert.

Papa said the flights were routine. "For we gunners its watching the anti-aircraft 'flak' going off (a black burst of smoke) below us, above us, hopefully never 'amongst us,' because that can ruin your whole day."

This is who my grandfather was. At the time, he had to marginalize the severity of such an event just to keep his sanity. Years later, he would joke about such things, I think in an effort to downplay exactly what he'd been through. He was a man who needed a sizable ego for his job, but never seemed to let it extend beyond that, at least not to me. Regardless of the epic scope of his life, Papa lived in the present as fully as anyone I'd ever known.

"My primary job on these missions was to fine tune the radar to get a max accurate 'picture' of the coast line."

One of the key islands in the area was Rabaul, which had previously been held by the British. After the Japanese attacked Pearl Harbor, the island had been evacuated in preparation for an attack. The British were correct in doing so, as the Japanese started bombing the island in January of 1942. By the time my grandfather would arrive at the islands, Rabaul had become a major base for the Japanese and home to more than 100,000 troops.

Instead of mounting a direct attack on the island, the Allied forces decided to set up airfields on the surrounding islands. "A more thrilling type mission we often did at Rabaul, on New Britain," wrote Papa. "It was a 'big' type base for the Japanese, so we raided it constantly."

The bombing was treacherous, though. "Low level, couple of hundred feet, called 'skip' bombing, into supply dumps, huts, ships in the water (if any), motor pools, anti-aircraft positions, etc. We lost our first aircraft and crew on one of those. Usually picked up a few machine gun .30 caliber holes in the aircraft, but no real damage to plane or us."

"You can hear hits," wrote Papa, "like a slap on the machine. Then things get a bit exciting. It gets even more exciting if that slap becomes a 'thump' with a shudder in the aircraft because that's a .20 millimeter round and far more potential."

I can just picture my grandfather a few thousand feet above the ocean, standing at the waist gunner spot, trying to locate his targets, trying to remember the radar readouts, and trying not to pay attention to the "slap" of machine gun fire. He was probably too focused on his duties to really worry about whether or not he'd suddenly hear a "thump" or a "shudder" instead.

One mission was later detailed by Staff Sergeant Lawrence McConkey in the public relations office. He interviewed Papa and sent a letter to the *Warren Tribune Chronicle* as something of a human interest story about the war. It seems like such articles were a regular part of what the military did back then, a way of showcasing the local boys who had made good:

How his pilot flew a Mitchell medium bomber 1,100 miles over water with one bad engine was related by Marine Sergeant Robert M.

Stuart, twenty-one, of Warren, Ohio, radio gunner returned from aerial action in the Southwest Pacific:

"It was a flight from Peleliu to Emirau," said the gunner member of a squadron called the "Forked Tailed Devils." "We flew all the way with a faulty right engine, all instruments and radio out of order. I sat in my seat and gritted my teeth, mentally pushing it all the way. I expected the engine to conk any minute, but we made it."

Returning to base, the Mitchell bomber crew continued their strafing and low-level bombing raids on Japs hemmed in the Bismark Archipelago. Chief targets were Rabaul and Kavieng. Sgt. Stuart completed 35 combat missions. His plane was damaged by flak twice, but not seriously.

Papa was stationed in the South Pacific for most of 1944, during which General MacArthur launched the campaign for the Philippines, specifically with the Battle of Leyte. The Marine Corps were brought in to supply a couple of fighter squadrons to suppress Japanese air activity. Papa's crew was assigned to fly navigation for a group of the fighters.

"We had to fly from Emirau to Hollandia to New Guinea where we joined up with the fighters," wrote Papa. "We spent the night at Hollandia where one crew member stayed with the airplane while the rest of us went up to the mountains to a Navy submarine rest camp. Our tail gunner Cosby got that duty. The Hollandia airfield was built on a swamp and loaded with mosquitoes so, sure enough, Cosby came down with malaria a couple of weeks later."

They later headed to Pelalu which had just been taken by the Marines in what my grandfather referred to as "a really nasty fight." They spent another night there, just a hundred or so miles away from Leyte.

When the Army invaded Leyte, the engineers bulldozed a stretch of beach to put down a couple thousand feet of PSP ("steel matting" says my grandfather) for a runway. While it's a great makeshift runway, it gets really slick when it rains.

Papa and his crew managed to land safe and sound, as did all the other planes they were flying with…except one. The plane skidded off the side of the strip, onto the beach, and into a "ball of scrap." The pilot was relatively unhurt.

"After the crash truck people pulled him from the remains," wrote Papa, "he came stomping into base operations madder than a wet hen and cursing very creatively as Navy types are wont to do."

Another major base for the Japanese was in the island group Chuuk, although it was known at the time as Truk. It served as Japan's main base in the South Pacific for both its navy and air force. Although the U.S. had done major damage to Truk during Operation Hailstone in February of 1944, it was occasionally still home to submarines, freighters, and other Japanese ships, as the majority of the Japanese fleet had been moved to Palau before the U.S. was able to launch its offensive.

Papa's squadron was assigned to make sure Truk was periodically swept clean so the Japanese weren't able to regain a foothold there.

"Now this was a real tricky operation," wrote Papa, "because it was at the absolute outer range of our ability to fly there, bomb, and fly home even with complete fuel consumption discipline."

I can only imagine what that last bit means. I would think that fuel consumption discipline would mean not taking any detours, but at the same time I can't imagine not having the option to change course if you're being fired upon. Again, my knowledge of these things comes mostly from Star Wars, but I would think the ability to engage in some kind of evasive action, even if just to avoid anti-aircraft and not actual planes, would be somewhat necessary. But I also can't see such a thing being taken into consideration if the target is so far away.

"Off we went, got there, made one pass over the bay and facilities dropping 'eggs' as we went. As I recall it, we flew at about two thousand feet cycling our bombs in pairs as we went. Hit anything? I have absolutely no idea as we had no fuel to make a second pass for a 'look see.' Got home with a few 'fumes' in the tanks."

They did get home, and in the first few weeks of 1945 crews started rotating back to the United States. The plan was to head back and begin more training in preparation for the "big show" as my grandfather would call it. "The big show" was the invasion of Japan.

My parents were here a few weeks ago. Appropriately enough, they stopped in Los Angeles for a few days on their way back from Hawaii, the site of America's entry into World War II and a place my grandfather would eventually end up stationed. His second child, my uncle Rob, would be born there.

While my parents were in town, Nicole and I drove them to visit some of my father's friends. Both were couples who were retired and had children and grandchildren. Of course there was lots of talk about what the future might hold for Nicole and me.

The subject of the book I was writing came up. And I found myself being able to talk about my grandfather's life with some semblance of knowledge. It was a strange position to be in because people were really interested in this, and I could tell that everyone was extremely impressed by the grandson who was writing a book about his grandfather's life. The fact that I had so much information to share—more than my mom, even— seemed to make everyone so happy, as if I was proof in some way that my generation was okay.

That's not to imply that I'm some sort of saint. It's taken me years to even start writing about my grandfather. A saint would have started this when his grandfather was younger and healthier. A saint would still be in Ohio.

My grandmother continued to send letters throughout 1944. She actually sent them to more soldiers than just my grandfather because she knew how important it was for them to know that people back home were thinking of them.

"Letters from military overseas were censored for content that might give information not for general knowledge," she wrote in her memoirs.

"Sometimes the letters were really marked up. But I kept writing to several different young men because letters from home were important to them."

Writing letters to servicemen was also a way for my grandmother to stay busy. Her father was still grieving the loss of his wife and grandma's sister, Eleanor, was worried about her own significant other, who was in the India Theater with Army Corps of Engineers.

"Looking back, it seems we could have been more supportive of one another during that troubled time," she wrote. That was difficult, though, with each of them having so much to worry about. I'm sure they each felt the loss of grandma's mom differently, too.

They did receive some good news: In March of 1945, Papa returned home, "looking so handsome and mature, having seen and done things beyond his years" as my grandmother would say. He came back with two air medals and a unit citation.

Papa's trip back had been just as interesting as his trip there. This time his ride home was an Army troop transport that had been heavily damaged by a kamikaze attack during the invasion of Leyte. The voyage back was a long one, but there was an upside. When the ship had been attacked it contained rations for a ship full of people. The boat was only 1/3 full as it headed back to the states and all rations were to be dumped when they reached San Francisco. Papa and his buddies were able to eat like kings.

"Mess hall was open 24/7," wrote Papa. "Remember, we hadn't been eating too well for a couple of days—days? Years!!"

After docking in San Francisco, it was off to San Diego for a week of debriefing and charm school "so you wouldn't say naughty words at the dinner table at home." It's funny to think that debriefing involved some level of training on how to behave in public. Yes, military secrets needed to be kept, but it was also important not to swear at the dinner table.

Papa then set off on the five day train ride back to Warren, Ohio. "Probably slept most of it, a skill I learned in the Marine Corps," he wrote. "If you have some open time, 'nap,' you may not get another chance for a day or two."

This thirty day leave was also when my grandfather renewed his relation-ship with my grandma. He arrived at the Davis house ready, it can be assumed, to sweep her off her feet. There was just one problem: she wasn't there.

"Since he wasn't expected that Sunday, I was not home," wrote grandma. "I was in Pittsburgh visiting a girl friend at Carnegie Tech. Eleanor told me how impatiently he waited for me. What a surprise to find him in my living room."

My grandmother continued "He lost no time transferring all the letter writing dreams into words and actions. I did have to work during the day, but my night school attendance at Youngstown College suffered."

By the time his leave was coming to an end, Papa was hoping for a commitment from grandma. But she wasn't ready. She was not yet 19, after all, and it had been less than a year since she lost her mother. While the thrill of having my grandfather back in the states must have been heady, it would have been a lot to process in a little time.

After his leave, Papa was sent back to California, to MCAS El Centro. There he started his re-training for the "Big Show."

"The concept was to be trained for a bird called the F-61," he wrote in a letter to an old Army buddy that he'd copied and sent to me, "a black, two engined, slick machine for night radar fighting and bombing." The plane was nicknamed the "Black Widow."

"Best thing I did was to convince your grandmother to come out to El Centro," Papa wrote in a letter to me.

As my grandmother said, "The letters between Warren and El Centro were very regular and soon it was just a matter of 'when' I would follow and we'd be married. He sent me a diamond ring, and I had his Dad put it on my finger."

Papa's parents were so involved, in fact, that grandma would end up taking the train to the base in El Centro, California with Papa's mom, who would be the only family member present at the wedding ceremony. They left Warren on Saturday, June 15, 1945 and would arrive the following Monday.

The day after she and her future mother-in-law arrived in El Centro,

Grandma and Papa bought their wedding rings. The next day was the rehearsal. Thursday, Papa had "night firing" drills. And finally, on Friday, June 22nd at 6:45 PM, my grandparents were married...

... For the first time.

After a brief honeymoon in Calexico, CA, my grandparents moved in to an apartment they shared with another Marine couple. This didn't last long, though, as the military decided to close the gunnery school in El Centro and move it to Opalocka Naval Air Station in Miami, Florida.

My grandfather says they were moved "lock, stock, and barrel." He then adds this: "Kyle, in case your sheltered education missed that term, back in small town 1800's stores changed hands lock (door), stock (inventory), and barrel (rain catcher on the corner of the building)."

There's something so very grand-parental about the fact that he told me that.

Papa moved out to Miami first and was able to find an apartment in a good section of town, although it was only a studio. That would soon become a problem, as not long after my grandmother arrived they learned she was pregnant.

"Plans moved too fast, we were too young and were caught up in an urgency," wrote grandma in her memoirs, "expecting that he would return to the Pacific and possibly a long hard fight against Japan."

"Had Mother been alive," she added, "things would have been different. More thought and sanity would have prevailed."

But Papa wouldn't have to return to the South Pacific any time soon. "Fortunately," he wrote, "because of our dropping two 'A' bombs, they quit and we didn't have to invade."

An end to the war meant an end to military service for many people and my grandfather was no exception. He was now a "surplus" soldier.

Grandma headed back to Warren while Papa waited for his discharge, making sure to re-enlist in the Marine Corps reserve to lock-in his sergeant stripes.

When Papa got to Warren he contacted what was then Western Reserve University (now Case Western Reserve) in Cleveland. He was accepted for enrollment in January, 1946 for a business degree on the GI Bill. This was just three months before my mom would be born.

Yet another newspaper clipping from this time announced a ceremony at the American Legion Hall in Warren where Papa and another Marine received citations. Papa was awarded an air medal and a gold star in lieu of a second air medal. There was even a dance held afterwards.

At the time, I don't think Papa really knew what to do with himself. I don't think he knew what life outside the military would be like. He wasn't quite twenty-two, yet he'd already spent three years in the Marines, fought the Japanese high above the Pacific ocean, and traveled to the other side of the world. Now he was married and expecting his first child in only a few months. Suddenly, he had to learn how to be a civilian.

In some ways that would prove harder than the war.

4

The Clock Starts Ticking

Tuesday, April 11, 2006

My mom called today. My grandfather is in the hospital. All indications are that his body is shutting down and there's ultimately not much to be done about it.

I don't know that I've been this upset about anything in a long, long time.

When I started writing the book about papa, I mentioned that writing it scares me. This is the exact quote from my journal:

"It scares me because the story of a life has one ending. And because I'm weird and pretentious and over educated and overly sensitive I worry that starting this written chronicle of Papa's life will parallel the real one. I worry that art imitates life. And I worry that there's only one ending to this book, an ending I don't like to think about and want to delay as long as possible."

And I know that it's not true. I know that it can't be. I know the universe is a cruel place, but it can't be that awful. But I also know that I'm a quarter of the way through the story of Papa's life. And I'm so mad at myself—mad that I didn't start this sooner. I'm so angry that I don't even know what to do.

I've spent the last three months submerging myself in Papa's life. It took me thirty years to finally stop being so self-absorbed and jaded about life so that I could take the time to look at my grandfather. It took me thirty years and I don't know why. And as of right now it looks like he won't be here to read it, won't even be here to help me finish it.

Why did I wait so long?

I was completely removed in 2002. I cried when my grandmother died and I cried when my uncle died and I was upset when my aunt died, although I didn't know her all that well. But I was in another state each time and I had distance. I only ever thought of those people when something came up. They were not in my head on a daily basis.

I've spent every day of the last three months thinking about Papa.

It's not fair. I know everyone says that when someone they love is dying or has died, but I'm going to be cliché and I'm going to say it anyway. It's not fair.

I think I cried more than Nicole has ever seen me cry before. I cried again in the shower. I started crying again just now.

I'm in Los Angeles and my grandfather is in a hospital bed in Ohio and there's nothing I could do even if I were there at this very moment.

I just want him to get better. I want something medically unheard of to happen and I want him to recover. I want his red blood cell count to increase and his kidneys to improve and the valve in his heart to get better. I want the sedatives to wear off and I want him to wake up and be better. And he'll get home and I'll call him and we'll talk for a few minutes and then he'll write me a letter while he's recovering. And he'll send me that letter and I'll work on the book some more while he's writing another letter. And this will go on and on until I'm done and we can see each other at the reunion and I can introduce him to Nicole and that's how the book will end. That's how it's supposed to end.

And sometime in the future he'll come to my wedding. And he'll meet my children. And the book will be a big hit and everyone will know just how amazing he is, what an incredible life he's led.

These are the things that have to happen because I honestly don't know what I'll do if they don't.

I'm tired. I'm tired of getting upset and I'm tired of crying and I'm even tired of writing. I'm going to go have a glass of whiskey and water and continue to send every positive thought I have to Ohio. Because it's really the only thing I can do.

Wednesday, April 12, 2006

So things could be much, much worse.

My mom called this morning to say that Papa is doing better. They've managed to get his red blood cell count up, which is good. I guess the cardiologist believes that everything would be fixed if they replace the valve in his heart. So they were going to see if he has a good night tonight and, if so, they're going to operate tomorrow.

Papa has been sedated through all of this, so it was grandma's decision to make. She said she wasn't sure if it was the right decision, but I think both my mom and I would have been really upset if she had decided against it. I guess Papa had been offered this surgery four years ago and passed on it.

Papa is 82, so this surgery is probably going to be tricky. I don't know how these things are worked out, but my mom gave me the impression that everyone is very optimistic. But, again, I don't know how much of that is accurate or just my family choosing the only line of thinking that's really open to them.

I spent all last night thinking "c'mon, Papa, fight this—we can't lose you yet. We still need you." I hope he heard me.

Next to this, everything else seems pretty trivial. I've put the book on hold just in case. I guess every little bit helps.

Thursday, April 13, 2006

Papa's blood pressure was low today and he had a bit of a fever, so the surgery is going to be tomorrow morning at five my time. It's a four hour surgery, so I should hear from my parents sometime there after.

Everyone thinks this surgery will do the trick, will fix a lot of his problems. But the fact remains that he's 82 and he's going to have a major operation performed on him. There are a lot of risks involved here.

So for another night I will be sending all my positive energy to him.

Nicole asked me today how it was that I'm able to handle this—all the waiting. And to be perfectly honest I'm not. I haven't slept well in the past few nights and I've mostly been subsiding on caffeine during the day and alcohol at night. I'm burning the candle at both ends because neither end is really helping me enough on its own.

Everything seems trivial and yet I wish I could focus on them. I wish I could focus on them because that would mean that Papa is fine.

Anyway, barring any further delays, my next entry should have some new information… and hopefully some good news.

Friday, April 14, 2006

Good Friday definitely was, although we're not all clear just yet.

Papa had his surgery this morning, which consisted of not just a heart valve replacement, but a bi-pass as well. That's an awful lot of work done on the heart.

They debated whether to go through with it or not this morning. Evidently his vitals (I say that as if I know what "vitals" consists of) weren't where they would have liked them to be. But basically the problem was that his heart wasn't pumping the quality of blood into his system that it needed and no amount of drugs was going to get him healthy enough to make the operation ideal. So they decided better to get his heart fixed and some good blood flowing than to wait any longer.

The doctor said the surgery went well and Papa is now in ICU. My parents are going to stay there in Dayton until Sunday. He's supposed to be off the respirator by then. My mom's going to drive back down again the following Thursday, the same day that my cousin is supposed to arrive, which is going to be kind of a mess. She just turned 17 and I don't know how much help she's going to be in this situation. I don't know.

I told my mom I'd been thinking about coming back to Ohio as soon as I can because I don't know that I want to wait the three months until the reunion to see Papa—or grandma, for that matter. We talked about it and decided I should wait a few weeks, though, as Papa has a pretty long road ahead of him. I know that he'd prefer to be close to back to normal if I came for a visit. That's going to be a while, though. He's not even supposed to leave ICU until the end of next week, and then he's got at least two more steps in the recovery process.

Basically, that all adds up to the fact that he still has a long way to go, so it's not time to open the champagne just yet.

This morning was kind of horrific for me, although I didn't have a major operation on my heart.

I was up pretty late with Nicole. I was drunk. It's weird, but drinking whiskey and water made me feel better for two reasons: one, Papa introduced me to that drink and two, it got me drunk. The argument could be made that getting drunk isn't the best way to deal with your emotions, but I like to think my superstitious yet sweet other reason for drinking makes up for that.

I haven't been sleeping well, anyway.

This morning was really bad. I knew Papa was supposed to go in for surgery at five AM LA time, so I kept looking at the clock thinking about how long it would be before he had the operation. I woke up around six and spent the next few hours half asleep, half awake, not just thinking about Papa, but also dreaming about him, or at least dreaming about different situations where I might find out the results of the surgery. In fact, I counted two positive results to one negative result in my dreams.

So there it is. Papa's over one hurdle, but we still have a long way to go. I think maybe I might be able to relax a little bit now, though. We'll see how I sleep tonight.

It's Monday, April 17th. Today is my mom's birthday. She called me while I was at work to give me an update on Papa.

"I'm supposed to call you today," I said.

"I just wanted to give you the latest on Papa," she said, "since I didn't call yesterday."

"I just figured no news was good news," I said.

And that was the case. Aside from Papa being a little more responsive and moving around a bit more, everything was still the same as when my mom had left.

"I keep forgetting it's my birthday," she said.

"Did you at least get to do something?"

"Yesterday we went over to your brother's for Easter and it ended up being a surprise birthday party," she said.

That was a good move by my brother. I don't know if that had been planned before Papa got sick, but it was a good move regardless.

"There's nothing coming from me," I said. And there wasn't, there isn't. I was going to send my mom flowers. I sent her flowers last year and she seemed to like them and I thought it was a nice gesture. I was actually going to order them Tuesday night, since I do that online. And then she called to tell me about Papa.

I couldn't imagine anything worse than having flowers sent to my mom. With everything so up in the air, I felt as if it would have been a bad omen.

"I didn't want to take any chances," I said.

"My mom said she was on the verge of breaking down, but then stopped herself because she thought she'd just lose it completely," I say.

Nicole is e-mailing her parents and her brother while I tell her this. She has updated them every single day on the condition of my grandfather. They've all sent messages back of sympathy and support.

"I think she was surprised at how upset I got," I say.

"She was," says Nicole, "I could hear her through the phone. I don't think she was expecting you to be that upset."

"You know," I say, "you can understand it a little bit because you live with me, but I don't think anyone can really understand what I've been doing for the past three months. I don't think anyone can understand just how engulfed in Papa's life I've become."

"I know," she says as she clicks on "send" and joins me on the futon. We don't have nice things at this point in our lives.

"Aside from grandma, I think I know things that no one else knows, or at least a combination of things that no one else knows."

"Your mom didn't even know about the divorce," says Nicole. This is another thing I love about her: I probably made reference to that conversation with Mom two months ago. Nicole doesn't think she has the ear for detail that I do, but she does. She's just not as neurotic as I am.

"Exactly," I say. "I feel like I'm finally starting to know him."

It's Tuesday morning and I'm late for work but I'm not that concerned. I was up late waiting for Nicole to get home from her new job (a night assistant editing job which has her there from 6:00 PM until anywhere from midnight to three in the morning) and drinking whiskey and water. Again, I know it might be stupid, but it makes me feel better. It makes me feel like I'm doing something.

A week before Papa went to the hospital my dad sent me an envelope full of various things: newspaper clippings about the Cleveland Indians, letters from my alma mater, and a copy of an article from the local paper. The article is a response to a study that was done to determine if praying for someone who's sick actually makes a difference.

I don't remember the details all that clearly, but there were a bunch of patients involved who all had the same illness and were being treated the exact same way. One group of patients was prayed for, although they didn't know it. A second group was prayed for and did know it. The final group wasn't prayed for at all (although the chances of that actually being maintained strike me as being slim to none). The end result of the study: the patients who were prayed for showed no difference versus those who weren't prayed for.

The article my dad sent me sought to refute the study, or at least offer that the power of prayer was unquantifiable. My dad felt the same way, although he also pointed out that the group performing this study got a grant for $12 million dollars and that I was in the wrong business.

I thought the study was fine, though. I just feel that it was backwards.

Prayer isn't for those being prayed for; it's for those doing the praying.

If you were to ask the friends and family that were allowed to pray if they thought their prayers had something to do with their loved one getting better, many of them would say yes. Some might say no. But if you asked them if praying made them feel better about the situation, made them feel like there was something they could do, some way they could contribute, then I would think that almost all of them would say yes.

I have no doubt that prayer works, but it's not meant to work on those who are sick.

Evidently, whiskey and water is my religion and I'll make a prayer every night until Papa is better.

"Kyle," says Nicole from the bedroom. I've just now gotten dressed for work. I've just now poured the last of my coffee down the drain.

"Yes?" I say as I walk into the bedroom. Nicole is lying on the bed with the first few chapters of this book spread out in front of her.

"I love it," she says. "It's great!"

I swear she doesn't always say that. She doesn't even normally say that. "Really?"

Nicole has always been kind enough to not pull any punches with me when she reads my writing. She liked the short story she read before this, but had problems with the ending, and told me as such. Often times her comments range from "I don't really understand what it's supposed to be about," to "I liked it," or "you're crazy." I get that last one a lot.

But I don't know that I've ever gotten such an enthusiastic response from her like this before, even when we'd first started dating and she had to humor me.

"Wow," I say because I'm a bit taken aback.

It was nice to hear, not just because she was stroking my ego, but because I felt like I was doing Papa justice.

It's Wednesday, April 19th, now and I got this e-mail from my mom:

Papa is off the ventilator! Very good news. Also he is off a bunch of tubes and sitting up in a chair. He is still not as alert but seems to be improving everyday. I would think he will go to a regular room soon. Tomorrow I go back for a few days. How long just depends on how things are going. Your Dad and Bosh are staying here. I'll call you from there with updates. Love, Mom

I should probably point out that Bosh is my parents' dog. I forwarded this e-mail to Nicole (as I was at work when I got it) who I'm sure then either forwarded it to her family or paraphrased it in an e-mail. It's so interesting to me that my family has suddenly become a part of hers. I don't know that I've ever had that happen to me before.

On Friday, Papa is going to be moved out of the ICU. This isn't just a huge relief, it is also somewhat surprising. Evidently he's come far enough that they felt safe moving him. He is no longer connected to any tubes and he's even managed to take a shower under his own power, or at least with only a nurse holding him steady. He still gets confused from time to time, but everyone seems to think that the longer he goes without any sedatives or painkillers in his system, the more and more alert he'll get.

After a week or two of rehab, he'll be able to go home again.

His surgery was a week ago. It seems like it's been so much longer.

I'm just waiting for the word that everything is okay, everything is stable, and that he's up for my visit. Then I'm buying my plane tickets home. Seeing Papa has never been more important. Finishing this book has never been more important.

5

Civilian Life, Take One

"WHEN DID THEY GET DIVORCED?" said my mom on the phone.

"In 1950," I said.

"See, I didn't know that."

My mom was fifty-nine when that conversation happened.

In February of 1950, my grandparents got divorced. They had been married for less than five years. My mom was not quite four. My mom was so young, in fact, that she never actually knew when they got divorced. She just assumed Papa was still going off on tours of duty.

I suppose there's a certain symmetry to it; my grandparents had a secret divorce and their daughter would end up having a secret marriage.

Back then, the state of Ohio required a one year grace period between the request for divorce and legal action, which meant that my grandmother actually filed in 1949.

Needless to say, the post-war years had not been easy.

As Papa started school in Cleveland in January of 1946, grandma stayed in Warren with her dad and her step-mother. Grandma was due in three months and the sixty miles between Cleveland and Warren must have seemed just as great as the distance between the United States and the South Pacific.

Four months after my mom was born, grandma moved up to Cleveland. At the very least, they would try to be a family, even if their circumstances seemed to be changing every few months.

But my grandparents had never been a normal couple. Their relationship had started, then stopped, then started up again through letters more than anything else. They weren't even face to face when grandma finally accepted Papa's proposal. When they were finally married, they were separated again not long afterwards. By the time they were together in Cleveland they had lived in three different places in three different states, no one place for any real length of time. On top of that, grandma got pregnant soon after the wedding, so most of their married life was spent preparing for the birth of my mom.

I don't know if any relationship could survive all of that. It's a testament to how much they cared for each other that they kept trying, particularly given how young they were.

A year after moving to Cleveland, grandma moved back to Warren to live with her family. Her father and step-mother had just had a baby boy, which meant that my mom's new uncle was actually a year younger than her.

Again, I can't imagine that situation was ideal, either. I'm sure my grandmother loved her dad and her step-mom, but the house had two babies in it, which had to have been a handful, even if, as I'm sure she'd tell me, my mom was the perfect baby. So after six months of this arrangement, and what I can only guess must have been a lot of talking with Papa, my mom and grandma moved in with Papa's parents, Seth and Goldie.

It's amazing for me to consider just how much time my grandparents spent living with their parents. Papa was twenty-three now, grandma twenty-one, yet they weren't able to go it alone on their own. It makes me think that, while parents are more likely to want their children to be self-sufficient at eighteen these days, children are much less likely to want to live with their parents. The idea of being twenty-three and moving in with my mom is completely foreign to me and I have nothing but love for my mother.

But a big factor in the beginning of my grandparents' relationship had been Goldie, Papa's mom. Grandma had lost her own mother at a young age, and Goldie helped to fill some of that void. As my grandmother wrote in her memoirs, "Probably I needed some mothering and she seemed willing to fill the need."

That close relationship only made their next challenge all the harder. In March of 1948, Goldie was diagnosed with tuberculosis.

Goldie was sent to a sanatorium to treat her TB. She was there for nine months, until December of 1948. She missed Papa's graduation that fall with a B.B.A. in marketing and a minor in economics.

I don't definitively know that Goldie's illness was the last straw, but it all began to add up. There was the strain of being apart again and the fact that Papa was in school while Goldie was being treated for TB. There was the fact that grandma was now left alone with her father-in-law, who, given his wife's condition, was probably little help in raising my mom. Then there was the simple fact that grandma and Papa had never been together on a regular basis for any real length of time. They'd never even really dated, so making the transition into married life was extremely hard. Eventually, the strain of those first few years after the war became too much and grandma filed for divorce.

It would be easy to see why my grandmother might be upset enough to want to end the marriage. It would be easy to paint my grandfather as the bad guy in that arrangement. But I think that would be inaccurate.

Imagine being twenty-three years old, having spent most of your adult life in the military, and suddenly having that taken away from you. There are rules in the military. There's a system. Life is black and white. It's not like that out here. In some ways I envy those who make the military their work because there's a simplification that comes with that, a kind of purity of thought that I don't think most people can understand.

I'm also sure that Papa was unable to talk to anyone about what he'd experienced in the South Pacific. My grandfather is a product of his generation (and his upbringing; we Midwesterners are notoriously close lipped) and is thus not very talkative, particularly when it comes to something so personal. These were things he probably couldn't share with his wife. I don't know that even his own father's experiences in France during the First World War would compare.

On top of that, grandma fell in love with a soldier—not just any soldier, but a Marine and a pilot to boot. There's enormous mystique to that. Papa's exit from the service was the first time the two of them really had a chance to get to know each other without extenuating circumstances. There are so many Baby Boomers for a reason: people met during war time and were swept away by the passion of the day. Bravery, fear, patriotism—it all mixed together to create something out of a romance novel.

But romance novels end.

The divorce served to underline one thing: Papa wasn't ready for the world outside the military just yet. So he did the only thing he could think to do: he re-upped.

Papa was working at Meehan Motors selling Studebakers when he made the decision to rejoin the military. There were no openings in the Marines at that time or, as my grandfather told an old Army buddy, "no billets in the corps, so (I) began the process of switching to the Army."

Grandma got custody of my mom, although I don't know that there was ever a formal hearing on the matter. I think it was probably always assumed that Mom would stay with Grandma, as she'd spent most of her life up until that point with just one parent around. Grandma stayed there in Warren with her parents. Papa would come and visit as often as he could.

Papa entered the Army as a 2nd lieutenant at Fort Knox, Kentucky in

Company A, 86th Tank as Armored Infantry. He later became company executive officer ("X.O.") and then 1st lieutenant A Company, Armored Infantry, all in the 3rd Armored Division.

But Papa wanted to fly. It was what he did.

He heard about Army Flight School at San Marcos, an Air Force Base which had just been reactivated in January of 1951. Papa would have to tough it out at Fort Knox, however, because it would take him nearly three years to get moved to San Marcos for Army Aviator training.

I don't know if it was the reality of raising a daughter on her own, or the rekindling of a long distance relationship, but at some point my grandmother started her relationship with Papa all over again.

I can't claim to have any real understanding of the social pressures that existed at that time, although Papa's parents were probably pushing for reconciliation between grandma and their son. Maybe Papa was able to get some kind of perspective back now that he was serving again. There could be any number of reasons. But whatever they were, the divorce was short lived.

On August 16, 1952, my grandparents got married. Again.

My grandmother doesn't give any details of the second wedding aside from the date and Papa never mentions it in any of his letters. The fact that they consider their anniversary to be the date of their first wedding says it all. To them, the divorce was just a bump in the road.

Unfortunately, any happiness their renewed romance might have brought was short lived.

On November 9, 1952, less than three months later, Seth Robert Stuart died from a heart attack. Intentional or not, my great grandfather set his son down the road of his military career, a road that would shape his entire life. Papa was only twenty-six when he lost his father.

A few months later Papa was transferred to San Marcos to begin Army Aviation training, a program that would eventually lead him to Korea.

While my grandfather is hesitant to talk about his tours of duty, he's less reticent when it comes to his days spent in training, particularly when those days involve the unbelievable events that make up a story he referred to as "The Ballad of Harvey Collins."

When Papa was stationed at Ft. Knox, Kentucky it was in a dry county. But forty miles north was Louisville, Kentucky, where drinking was completely legal. Highway 41 runs through Ft. Knox and into Louisville. From the way my grandfather tells it, as soon as you cross the county line into Louisville the highway is paved by miles of sleazy bars "inhabited by soldiers and equally sleazy 'farm' girls."

One day there was an article in the local paper saying that the remains of one of these girls had been found in an abandoned well. The authorities were looking into it, but they had no suspects.

"Fast forward," says Papa in a letter, "I go off to fight school at San Marcos." He mostly stayed on the base then, spending his evenings with his class friends at the officers club. In another class was a captain who also came from Knox. Papa described him as "a strange sort of guy who keeps trying to join our group."

Behind San Marcos there were nursing quarters, set up a lot like an old motel. One night someone snuck into the nurses quarters and, as my grandfather said, "beats the daylights" out of one of them. Of course there was another investigation (this is on Army soil now, after all), but again there were no suspects. Papa graduated and headed to Ft. Sill, Oklahoma for three months of operations training on L-19 aircraft.

Well, one night Captain Harvey Collins stole an L-19 and flew back to Texas. He left a suicide note behind. He landed on some railroad tracks, in theory to do himself in, but he didn't actually kill himself: he simply disappeared.

Eventually, he was found, captured, court marshaled, and tossed out of the Army. But, of course, the story doesn't end there.

"Seems Harvey is nuttier than a fruitcake," wrote Papa.

Harvey holed up in a motel room in Seattle with a samurai sword (yes, a samurai sword) and proceeded to kill a few people. He's captured yet again, this time tried and convicted for murder—and sentenced to hang.

But the "Ballad of Harvey Collins" couldn't have such a mundane ending. Harvey managed to escape from jail, which led to a large manhunt. They found him rather quickly, though, although his escape succeeded in doing one thing: speeding up his execution. He didn't have a chance to escape the second time around.

"So ends the Ballad of Harvey Collins," wrote my grandfather. "But later, Harvey even made a big spread in the 'True Detective,' a very popular magazine at the time."

In the spread it's revealed that, while awaiting execution, Harvey admitted to killing the woman in Kentucky and beating up the nurse in Texas.

Said my grandfather: "You meet such interesting people in the Army!"

6

Complications

I SHOULD BE GETTING ON A PLANE for South Korea right now. I should have already flown over those obscure islands in the South Pacific. I should have visited the sites that used to house Japanese bases. I should have sweated out Florida and North Carolina, a short stint in California and a brief stay in Mexicali. I should have been able to walk down that street in Warren, Ohio where Papa grew up. I should have gone to the park where he and my grandmother first met. But I haven't, I won't, and I can't. I don't have the time or the money. And, as sad as this might sound, I don't think I'd be able to be away from Nicole for that long.

I don't know how my grandparents did it. I don't know how they spent so much time apart, let alone spent that time not knowing if they'd ever see each other again. I can't imagine living with that uncertainty, that anxiety that builds in the pit of your stomach when you try to imagine your life without the other person.

It's no wonder they eventually go re-married.

No, aside from the time and the money, I could never leave Nicole to travel around the world. But I would love to take her with me.

Papa is going home.

"They think it might be the blood thinner," said my mom, giving me the latest reason for why his red blood cell count is still low. It seems that a drug he's taking to help with one problem might actually be causing another.

"But it's definitely not his bone marrow," my mom assured me. This, in itself, is a relief. None of the diseases I looked up that were connected with bone marrow problems were mild, to say the least. I feel like we're making a list of all of my grandfather's parts and just going down and checking off the ones that are okay. Bone marrow? Check.

The fact that my grandfather is going home is even more reason to rejoice. His low blood cell count was a problem, yes, but it wasn't something that was keeping him from returning to normal. He was still recovering from the surgery, of course, but he was making steps towards getting back on his feet. Since the low red blood cell count wasn't directly effecting how he felt, lying in a hospital bed for days seemed like cruel and unusual punishment.

Papa would actually tell me as much when I called the next day. He said that being the in hospital felt like "being locked in jail even though I didn't do anything wrong."

That phone conversation was typical of both of my grandparents. The entire call couldn't have lasted more than six minutes, split evenly between the two of them.

My grandmother answered the phone and after a brief response to "how are you doing?" started talking about all the rain they were getting. She then pointed out to me that the weather in Northern California has actually been warmer than the weather in Southern California. Then she asked how Nicole was doing. Then she asked how Nicole's dad was doing, as he'd recently had a quadruple bi-pass (he's doing fine, by the way). Notice how the entirety of my conversation with my grandmother consisted of her talking about anything other than herself.

She did, however, tell me that Papa's blood thinner medicine was rat poison, which I thought was funny and I told her I'd put that in the book.

Papa was the same way. He never really talked about how he was feeling, aside from how restless he got in the hospital. He mentioned how he hoped to be well enough to drive up to see my parents, my brother, and the grandkids soon. He said that as soon as he conquered the stairs to the basement he was going to get the hand held tape recorder I'd gotten him and start recording more information for me. He said that writing is too hard for him right now.

I told him not to rush things, that the tapes could wait until he was up to it. He said he needed something to do.

In fact, this is the reason why I've yet to fly back to Ohio.

After a few e-mails and phone calls with my parents, it became clear that flying to Dayton specifically to see Papa was going to cause some problems. First and foremost was the fact that my grandmother is 80 years old, and yet feels the need to do things like prepare full meals for anyone who visits. Basically, any visit from me or anyone else would be an added burden to her workload, which already consisted of taking care of Papa.

A bigger issue was the fact that I would visit for a few days and spend most of that time tape recording a conversation with Papa. In the span of forty-eight hours I would more or less get all of the information I needed to finish writing this book. That would be well and good as far as the time table on this book is concerned, but it would then leave Papa with nothing to occupy his time—a point he underlined when we talked on the phone.

Instead it was decided that I would pick another time to come home, like when my grandparents finally make the move closer to my parents. Then I could visit and I could help them move—I could be of some use to them. Still, I had no idea when that would be. I had no idea how long I'd have to wait.

But today in the mail I received the details for the family reunion in July. So at the very least I'll get to see him in a few months.

I've also realized that I need to call more often.

I had no idea just what a classic example of my grandparents—of my family—that phone call had been until I talked to my mom four days later.

"Grandma said you called on Thursday?" she said.

"Yeah, late afternoon, I'd say."

"She didn't mention that she and Papa had been in the emergency room all day?" This was really more of a statement coming from my mother as she knew what my answer was going to be.

"What?" I said. Neither of my grandparents had come anywhere close to even insinuating that they'd been within a fifty mile radius of any kind of medical establishment, let alone that the paramedics had been at their house—which, evidently, they had.

My mom explained to me that my grandfather had started to lose feeling in his arm. My grandmother was running some errands, so he called 911. The visiting nurse arrived during that time as well, so my grandmother returned to quite a scene.

They went to the emergency room where it was determined that the blood thinners that my grandfather had recently stopped taking were actually the one thing preventing him from having a stroke. So they decided to start him on them again, but at half the dose he'd been taking before.

"Grandma said the only reason she even told me about it is because Papa's taking the blood thinners again, so eventually she'd have to explain that." Basically, the drug trail was going to eventually cause someone to ask, which is why grandma said something—a pre-emptive strike so she wouldn't have to go into detail later.

"Are you serious?" I said, although I suppose I was just going through the motions of shock. I shouldn't have been surprised at this. God forbid my grandparents bother anyone with their problems. Honestly, god forbid anyone in my family bother anyone, even people who care about them.

"They were there until 4:30," she said.

"I probably called them at five," I said. They'd been home for a half an hour. I was probably the first person they talked to when they got home. And yet they never let on that anything out of the ordinary had happened.

But the news seemed to be positive and Papa's new dosage should take care of both problems. He should have more red blood cells and still remain stroke free.

Still, the extent of my family's desire to not make waves has given me a new perspective on this book. Not only will this be a fitting tribute to the life my grandparents had together, but it could also stand as a fairly atypical, detailed chronicling of my family. This book could be the most open any of us has ever been.

I once tried to explain to someone that writing a book involves giving up any semblance of control; you don't write the book, the book writes you. As of this moment, I'm not getting the ending I'd planned. Papa is doing better, but neither of us will be going to the family reunion in July.

My reasons for going to the reunion were threefold: to see my grand-parents and my nephews, for Nicole to meet those same people, and to show Nicole around Atlanta, a city I called home for two years. In the span of the last few days, however, most of those reasons have been taken off the list.

My brother and his wife don't think that my four year old nephews, who have been through a lot in their brief stay on this earth, will behave themselves long enough for a flight to Atlanta, let alone navigating an airport and staying in a hotel. So that branch of my family tree won't be going.

Papa was in the hospital again last weekend, again trying to get his mix of medications right. He's having less serious complications, though, mostly involving swelling in his legs. His heart sounds great, but he still needs to take things slowly. He also needs to be close to his doctors. And while Papa thinks he'll be ready to go to the reunion by the end of July, my grandmother is less optimistic. As of right now, chances are good that they'll stay home.

The only real reason left to go to Atlanta would be to show Nicole around the city, but I could do that any time or, more specifically, any time other than the summertime. Atlanta summers can be oppressively hot.

With the reunion out of the picture the question now becomes: when do I end this?

"Maybe," says Nicole.

"Really?" I say. I'm completely shocked by this.

"Well, my cousin's baby will only be a few months old, so if there's ever a Christmas where I won't miss much, it will be this one."

"Seriously?" I'm still stunned.

"You came home with me last year," she says, "I should do the same for you."

I had never in a million years thought Nicole would go back to Ohio with me for Christmas. I know that my mom was strongly pushing for such a thing, but I just couldn't picture it. Holidays mean a lot to Nicole. She's also a native Californian, so cold weather, truly cold weather, is something of a foreign concept to her.

"My dad said something to me the last time I was home," she says, "that they expected me to spend this Christmas with your family."

"Are you going to be able to do that?" I say. "I mean, I got choked up on Christmas Eve because I was away from home and the holidays aren't even a big deal for me."

"Oh, it's going to be hard," she says. "But if there's ever a year for me to do it, it's this one."

"Wow."

"Maybe," she says. "Just remember that it's still a 'maybe.'"

My first novel took me a year to write.

"If we don't go to the reunion, Christmas will have to be my ending."

"That would be perfect," says Nicole. "Then it would be one full year from when you started."

There's that symmetry again.

I think I've been rushing this and now that I physically can't rush it I almost feel like I can actually enjoy it a bit more. I've had such an intense drive to research and write this book that slowing down might be exactly what I needed to let it grow as it should. Perhaps I've been forcing the matter.

"You know," I say, "if we don't go to Atlanta then we could go to Ohio instead and we could go at any time—we could go when you're in between seasons at work and then we'd have some time."

"That'd be great," she says. I've seen all the important places in Nicole's life. I've been to the street she lived on until she was six. I've been to the house she lived in after that. I've been to her alma mater and driven past her first apartment in Los Angeles. Because my history is on the other side of the country, she's been unable to see any of it. I can tell she's excited to get the chance.

There it is: We're going to Ohio. At the beginning of July, when Nicole has a week off, we're going to Ohio. I'm going to see my nephews. I'm going to see my grandparents. I'm going to sit down with Papa and talk about the book. He's going to hand me the tapes he's finished so far and I'll promise him that this book is doing him justice.

Papa grew up in Ohio. He met my grandmother there. His children call it home. It's where he chose to retire.

All signs point back to Ohio.

7

Ohio

"I CAN'T BELIEVE WE'RE GOING to Ohio," I say.

"I can't believe we're going to Ohio, either," says Nicole.

We'd been saying this on and off for weeks, and now we were saying this as we boarded our flight from LAX to Cleveland. We decide that Christmas was too long to wait, so we were heading to Ohio now, in July. This was to be my first visit home since last September, and Nicole's very first trip to my hometown. She was finally going to get to meet my friends from high school, my brother's wife Wendy, their twin boys Nathan and Connor and, of course my grandparents.

I've taken a good amount of time off from writing this book. My grandfather's medical problems have him going in and out of the hospital on a fairly regular basis. His doctors are still unable to figure out why his red blood cell count keeps falling. They are giving him regular blood transfusions as a temporary fix, but that can't go on forever. They need to find the source of the problem.

In all other respects, though, it seems that his surgery has been a success; his new heart valve is performing as it should, fairly amazing in and of itself considering Papa is eighty-two years old. He'd lost some weight since he first became ill, but he seems to be in good spirits whenever I talk to him. He just seems frustrated that he's spending so much time in hospitals.

"This is a 737," I say to Nicole. "My grandfather will ask when we see him. And then you'll learn more than you ever wanted to know about the 737."

Flying across the country usually makes me nervous, but not this time. This time I'm flying home with Nicole. This time I'm going to end up in Ohio with most of the people I truly care about in one place.

"Thursday you can take one of our cars down to Dayton to see grandma and Papa," says my mom. "We're not going to meet them halfway because Papa's in the hospital again."

The plan had been that Papa was going to use my trip as a gauge on his wellness. We were going to drive half way from Kent to Huber Heights, Ohio and meet them at a Bob Evans for lunch. This way Papa would be able to get out of the house and on the road, something he very much missed. He liked being self-sufficient.

But his red blood cell problem has forced him to return to the hospital again and even if he would be out by Thursday (we arrived in Kent on Sunday night), he'd be in no condition to drive anywhere.

"That's about seven hours round trip," says my mom, "but you're young."

"Will he be home by then?" I say.

"Well, every day they keep saying he might be able to go home and every day they end up keeping him, so I'm not really sure," she says.

"That's got to be driving him nuts."

"He keeps telling them that he just has to be home by Thursday— that his grandson from California is coming to see him."

"I can see him just as well at the hospital," I say.

"Do you have questions for him?" says my mom. She and Nicole and I are sitting at the kitchen table. My dad is in the adjacent living room.

Nicole and I are eating breakfast. My parents have eaten long ago as it's now after noon.

"You know, Nicole asked me that, too, and I really don't," I say. "I mean, what would I ask him? 'Can you sum up Vietnam in a few sentences for me?'"

Everyone laughs.

"Just give me something pithy," I say.

"Just a few quotes—something flashy," says Nicole.

While I'd love to sit down with Papa over a few drinks and a tape recorder, we could very well be seeing him at the hospital. Since I started writing this book, Papa has only ever shared stories about the wars he fought in when asked about it and even then those are mostly vague and humorous anecdotes. I can't see him going into a staggering level of detail when we meet.

I had been hoping Papa would show up with audio tapes in hand, but my grandma had told me in an e-mail that he hadn't felt up to recording himself yet. And of course this wasn't my concern. While there might have been a time at the beginning of this book when I was anxious to complete it as quickly as possible, that thought had taken a back seat to my desire to see my grandfather get better. I would spend the next decade writing this book if it meant he'd be around.

No, this trip isn't about the book. It's about seeing Papa again for the first time in almost a year. It's about Nicole finally getting to meet the man I have spent so much time talking about for the past six months. It's about hopefully giving him the strength he needs to finally beat this health problem.

I know how egotistical that must sound. But I really believe that seeing him again will help. I know it will help me, will re-energize me for my return back to Los Angeles. And for some reason I feel like I can do the same for him.

My time in Ohio is well planned.

Nicole and I arrived Sunday night. Monday night we went to an Indians game. Tuesday night we celebrated the 4th of July at my brother's house. Tonight, Wednesday night, we are going to my friend Anne's house for a potluck. All of my friends from high school are going to be there.

While Nicole had already met my brother and my parents when they visited Los Angeles, she had a fairly long list of people waiting for her in Ohio. Before the baseball game on Monday she met my brother's wife, Wendy, and finally got to meet my twin nephews. While family may not play as pivotal a role in my life as it does for many, my nephews are different. They are perhaps my favorite people in all the world regardless of what they might do. Yes, I could point to the fact that they are miracle children (and I'll get to that later). But that's not it. To be honest, I'm not entirely sure I can explain all the reasons why my nephews are so important to me. It goes beyond a simple love for my brother's children. In some ways I think it stretches into symbolism, that these two boys represent all that's good in the world.

Leading up to the potluck at Anne's, Nicole had met all but one of my friends from high school, although she'd never hung out with them all at once. I mentioned before that one of the familial traits I inherited was an amazing ability to be alone. This talent also means that the friends I do make end up sticking around for a long time. I had been friends with this particular group for 13 years. We hadn't seen each other on anything of a regular basis for 12 of those. That's how amazing these people are.

Over the course of the first few days in Ohio, I'd mentioned to my mom this blueberry concoction she used to make me for my birthday. We'd managed to determine that it had been at least ten years since she'd made it and she was actually a little fuzzy on exactly what had gone into it.

That's why my mom is flipping through her box of recipes when the phone rings.

Nicole is helping me bag comic books to take back with me to Los Angeles, but at the moment my hands are free. Since my mom is busy flipping through index cards, she asks me to answer the phone.

"Sure," I say as I jump up to grab the cordless phone off the wall.

"Hello?"

"Is this Kyle?" It's grandma.

"Is this grandma?" I say. We always do this.

She's calling from the hospital.

"Papa's dressed and we're all packed, we're just waiting for the paper-work," she says.

They still don't know what's causing the low red blood cell count. All tests have come back negative. Their current plan of action is to make sure he gets a transfusion every six weeks while continuing to search for the source of the problem.

No one is particularly happy about this.

Grandma tells me she's going to make salmon quiche for lunch to-morrow. I tell her we'll probably get there between 12:30 and 1:00.

"Well, just call when you get close," she says.

It's a little strange talking to my grandmother, planning our visit. While not particularly mushy, nor kept on a daily basis, my grandmother's mem-oirs still seem fairly private. I feel like I've spent the last few months going through her diary.

"How's Papa doing?" I say.

"Here, let me get him for you," she says.

I hear her pass off the phone.

"Hi, Kyle," says Papa.

Papa always answers the phone this way when he knows it's me. At some point he usually calls me "dear heart," a phrase I've only ever heard him use. It's a term I've never thought about before, but one that fits him perfectly. My mom, the twins, my family, me—we're all dear hearts to him.

He tells me that he has too many doctors and that even if one of them thinks they know what's best, the others have to put their two cents in.

"Every day they say that I'm going to get to go home," he says. "And then they tell me I have to stay."

He sounds good. I can tell that he frustrated, but otherwise he sounds healthy.

I can tell that he's happy to be going home. There's something there, in his voice, in the way that we're talking. Our words might be focused on doctors and hospitals and the like, but there's more to it than that. In many ways it feels like my visit is the only thing in the world to either of us right now. After all the letters and the e-mails and the phone calls and the health problems and the change of plans, it seems like this visit is going to be a reset button of sorts, a new beginning. I've yet to see him face to face since I started digging into his life. We've yet to sit in a room together since I began submerging myself in his personal history. Our relationship has changed over the past few months yet we've never seen each other during that time.

This was going to be new.

"Would you like to talk to mom?" I say. Papa, as usual, didn't want to keep me on the phone. He never wants to trouble anyone.

"Yes, let me talk to your mother," he says.

I pass the phone off and sit down next to Nicole, explaining to her the situation.

We should probably get ready for the potluck soon.

It's amazing how far we've come.

My friends don't get together like this. Honestly, they only do so when I'm in town and I come to town so rarely. But here they are now, just like it used to be. I graduated from high school twelve years ago, yet here they all are.

It's changed, of course. Of the five of us, three are married and two of those three have children. We all have significant others. This isn't a private club anymore and I wouldn't have it any other way. While I'll admit that there's some sadness to the fact that we don't have moments like this anymore, there's comfort in knowing that all of us are loved, that all of us have someone in our lives.

At one point one of my friend's parents arrive, taking advantage of this rare gathering to see a group of people they used to see so often.

As always, questions abound about my life in Los Angeles. And while

I dance around the mundane aspects of my every day existence, I concentrate on what really matters most to me: my life with Nicole and the book that I'm writing about my grandfather.

"I'm writing a book about my grandfather," I say. I get positive responses from this, but nothing off the charts seismically.

"He fought in three wars," I add and suddenly the response is one of awe. I suppose books on octogenarians aren't unusual. It's pretty clear, however, that books on three war veterans are. I never even get around to telling them about my grandfather's roller coaster love affair with my grandma.

I find that writing this book has turned me into one of those people. Not unlike a born again Christian, I'm filled with an enthusiasm for my chosen passion that is almost impossible to explain to anyone who isn't me. And while everyone from my best friends to Nicole's parents shows a certain amount of reverence for what I'm doing, none of them can truly understand how deeply it's affected me or how all encompassing the process has become. Nicole is the only one who can even come close to any level of comprehension, and I think that's due to equal parts her exposure and how much she understands me.

There was a point when my friends and I would head to the bars as soon as I arrived in town. Now we have a potluck. We drink wine. We watch the kids play and comment on how cute they are. And this all makes me just as happy—if not more so—as if we were doing shots until dawn.

The downside, of course, is that children have bedtimes and their parents must abide by those bedtimes. So, sooner that I would like, people begin leaving.

It's just as one of my friends is preparing to go that my cell phone rings.

I pull it out of my pocket. It says that Parents' Cell is calling.

Had I not had so much wine, I probably would have wondered why my parents were calling from their cell phone and not their home line. Had I not had so much wine, perhaps I would have wondered why they were calling me at all. It was just after ten and I can't imagine that they were concerned about my whereabouts. Perhaps they were worried I wouldn't be able to get up early tomorrow for the trip to Dayton.

Regardless, I answer the phone.

"Hello?" I say.

"Kyle? It's Dad. Your mom's on the other line." I wonder if he thought in advance to explain that to me or if it just came naturally to him.

I still can't believe that I just answered the phone. I never stopped to consider what I would get on the other end.

"Papa died," he says. "You need to come home."

8

Aftermath

THIS IS WHAT PEOPLE DO when someone dies: they make plans.

One of my brother's twin sons, Connor, has surgery tomorrow to have his tonsils removed and to have tubes placed in his ears. Since he and his parents need to be at the hospital extremely early in the morning, his brother Nathan is staying with my parents for the next twenty-four hours, or at least that had been the plan up until now.

"Grandma Sherry is crying," said Nathan earlier as my mom tried to put him to bed. Her crying was making him cry, so she was forced to compose herself to get him to go to sleep.

"Isn't Megan supposed to fly in on Tuesday?" says my dad. Megan is my cousin, my only cousin, and she's very close to my grandfather. She's very close to him because both of her parents are dead and grandma and Papa have been the only major link she has to this side of her family. She spent time with my grandparents every summer, and her latest visit was to start this Tuesday.

"Jesus," I say.

He just wanted to make it home by Thursday. He just wanted to make it home so he could see his grandson who was visiting him from California.

"I can't imagine the funeral will be before Monday," says my mom and I can't believe she's talking about her father's funeral. I can't believe that I'm sitting in my parents' living room in Ohio and I'm having a conversation about when my grandfather's funeral is going to be and how long I'll have to extend my trip to make sure I can be there.

We were just fifteen hours away from seeing him.

Nicole opens a bottle of wine. She pours my mom a glass. It's a bottle that Nicole and I will finish off by ourselves as my parents get ready for bed, get ready for the morning to come.

After my dad called, I said "okay" into my cell phone then promptly threw it away from me, as if it had just tried to attack me. I stormed into Anne's backyard, taking her screen door off the track as I did so. I stopped behind a car and squatted down. Tears were building up in my eyes, but never came down.

Nicole was by my side almost immediately.

"Is it your grandpa?" she said.

"He's dead."

We spent the next half an hour inside with my friends, drinking wine. Eventually we made our way back to my parents' house.

And now we're lying in bed in my old bedroom, a room which has long since lost any resemblance to what it was over a decade ago when I called it my own. We're lying in bed and I'm drunk on wine and I honestly have no idea what to do with myself.

Nathan's other grandmother takes him in the morning. My mom heads to Dayton that afternoon. I ask her if she'll be okay and she tells me that the drive will do her some good. My dad, Nicole, and I are to follow the next day, after we've made all the necessary arrangements for our extended stay.

I spend most of the day on the phone and online. We have bosses to call, friends to call, an airline to call. I send a mass e-mail to the extended family letting them know what has happened and that the funeral service will be Monday morning.

Nicole and I pack that night because this is the last we'll see of my parents' house; we'll leave for Los Angeles directly after the funeral. I have a knot in my stomach and I don't know that I've ever been so hesitant to leave my parents' house.

I'll admit that I just want to go back to Los Angeles. I want to run away. I know that it's unhealthy and in many ways cowardly, but living so far away from my family and friends places me in a position where I don't have to live with family drama on a daily basis. When someone dies it hurts, but it's not something that sticks with me every day because I don't have any reminders of them like that. When my uncle died it was horrible for a number of reasons, but I saw him for maybe four days out of the year. In my head, for the other 361 days in a year, he is alive and well and I just don't see him.

I just want to run back to Los Angeles so I can forget all about this. But I know that it's not possible, not this time, not with my grandfather. He has become too much a part of my life for me to escape this.

We reschedule our flights for Monday night. We drive down to Dayton on Friday morning.

My grandmother slips from sad to fine in the span of seconds.

"Grandma, what can I do?" I say. Right now it's just the immediate family. Those who are coming in early will arrive on Sunday.

"Just be sweet," she says as she pats my hand. "Just be sweet."

In many ways I think this is how my grandfather saw me, too. I was the youngest, the most prone to flights of fancy, and I think my grandparents viewed me as being something of a free spirit, but not so much so that I was irresponsible. Maybe they knew how emotional I could be. Maybe they just assumed the fact that I was a writer meant I viewed the world differently than most.

"He tried so hard," she says as she continues to pat my hand, "he tried so hard to get home to see you."

She starts to cry and I pat her hand in return. "I know," I say.

This should have had me in tears, but this moment isn't about me. Right now, I feel like crying would be selfish. These next few days are about grandma, and about my mom. They're not about me.

"Here you go, mom," says my mom as she hands grandma a piece of paper. Grandma has slipped back to being fine again. I suppose that's inaccurate; she's only fine on the surface.

"Thank you, dear," says Grandma as she sets the piece of paper on the counter in front of her.

There's a breakfast bar in my grandparents' kitchen. Grandma is on the kitchen side of it, standing up. I'm on the dining room side of it, sitting in a bar chair. It's something I've done for as long as I can remember; they've been in this house for nearly forty years. The plan, as of this moment, however, is that Grandma will sell the house and move up to Kent to be closer to my parents.

It dawns on me that when I leave on Monday I will never see this house again.

I look down at the piece of paper my mom just gave to my grandma. It's Papa's discharge paper. I pick it up and look it over.

Robert Merwin Stuart.

"Goldie and Seth couldn't decide on a middle name, so they named him after the doctor that delivered him," says grandma.

Box 24 under Service Data lists "Decorations, Medals, Badges, Commendations, Citations, and Campaign Ribbons Awarded or Authorized". The list is fairly long.

"The medals are probably around here somewhere," says grandma.

"Do you think I could have a copy of this?" I say.

"They're going to make a copy at the funeral home," she says. "You can have this one when I bring it back. I'm sure I have another copy somewhere. I've got a bunch of old photos I can give you, too."

"Anything you want to send me, anything you think I could use, I'd love to have," I say.

"I will," she says. "You're the next generation; no sense in me keeping it." She pats me on the hand again.

"It's good," she says as she smiles at me. "It's good that you're interested in these things."

"Thank you for staying," I say.

"Of course," says Nicole. I don't really know what I'd be doing right now if she hadn't decided to stay.

We're lying in bed in a hotel room. This room has been something of a godsend for us, as it's become a sanctuary. In this hotel room we can actually be alone for a little while. We can just be together and put everything else on hold, if only for a few hours.

Huber Heights—the suburb of Dayton where my grandparents live—is a small town and the complete darkness and lack of white noise is unsettling.

"You haven't really reacted yet," says Nicole. "I want to make sure I'm with you when you do."

"I know," I say. "Honestly, I don't know that it will happen until I get back to Los Angeles and write about all of this."

"You don't have to hold it in for that," she says.

"I'm not. Believe me, I'm not. It's just that right now I keep thinking about my grandma. I didn't see Papa that often, but grandma spent every day of her life with him for sixty-one years. How do you deal with something like that changing completely?"

"I hope I go first," says Nicole. "Because I don't think I could handle that."

"I wouldn't want you to."

The CD player on my laptop is playing. The speakers are not the best, but we needed some kind of music, some kind of noise to help us fall asleep.

Nicole drifts off to sleep, her breathing getting heavier as she loses consciousness. The Postal Service is playing, a song called "We Will Become Silhouettes," the last song on the album. My mind had been wandering, but comes back to the music in time for the final chorus: "We will become silhouettes when our bodies finally go."

The night before my other grandmother's wake, I had a dream about her. I wonder if I'll dream about Papa.

9

Funeral

WE ARE THE FIRST FAMILY MEMBERS to arrive at the church.

It's an open casket service.

There's a moment after we've arrived when we are meeting various church members and signing the guest book and picking up the folded pieces of paper that will lead us through the service where everything seems to stop. Someone has hit the pause button.

I know that in the main hall of the church, towards the back for the hour that makes up the viewing, is a casket holding my grandfather, my Papa. I know that his lifeless body is lying in a box and that I am expected to walk up to him, to look at him, and to say my goodbyes. It is expected that seeing him there, seeing him dead, seeing him the one way I never, ever want to remember him will give me some sort of closure.

I suppose the options are to see him one last time or to never see him again. But I don't know that seeing him one last time like this is really the better choice.

Grandma begins to cry as soon as she sees him. He looks very pale.

My mom begins to cry as soon as she sees him.

My dad comforts my mom. My brother and I comfort my grandma. Nicole stands at the ready to comfort me. After a few moments, I turn away and walk a few steps towards the other end of the church.

My arms are folded across my chest and Nicole will later tell me that she knew this to mean that I was more angry than sad. And at that moment I was. Because I shouldn't be in that church, I shouldn't be looking at my dead grandfather's body. None of this should have been happening.

And yet it was.

Nicole and I go out to the antechamber and soon distant relatives and family friends begin arriving. I would hazard to say that at least 90% of them are elderly.

I point that out not to be dismissive or mean, but simply because this meant that 90% of those in attendance have a different view on the proceedings than I. They are sad, yes, but there is no anger there, there is no frustration. This is the natural order and to them this is acceptable. To me it is not.

My dad comes by and asks if I've seen my brother. I tell him that I saw him go outside not too long ago. It seems that my dad and my cousin's aunt looked for him but were unable to find him.

I head outside, knowing full well that my brother and I, although six years apart in age, still have a lot in common. We don't share these things with others. It's just not what we do, save, I suppose, in a book about our family.

I find Chris just around the corner of the building. He's heading back towards the door into the church. It's pretty clear that seeing Papa has upset him. It's upset all of us.

"Hey," he says as I walk up to him.

"Hey," I say as I give him a hug. We're not a family that generally hugs. But this isn't something that generally happens.

"Dude," he says, "you're too freaking tall."

We head back inside and run into my dad, then Nicole.

We spend the next half an hour meeting various people, all of whom give us their condolences. Word gets around that Nicole is my fiancé because that's how my grandma has been introducing her. She thinks it sounds better that way and at this point I'm inclined to do whatever she wants.

My mom comes up to me as I sit on a bench sandwiched between Nicole and my cousin Megan. I've just gotten through telling Megan that we should start e-mailing each other and that she comes from a long line of strong women.

"Grandma wants you," says my mom. "I think she wants to show you off."

I suppose that makes sense. I'm the grandson from California and I'm writing a book about Papa. I'm his living legacy. It's only right that grandma would want people to know who I am.

Nicole and I get up and head back into the church. Grandma has spent the entire hour of the viewing standing by Papa's casket.

I put my arm around my grandma as she introduces me to the pastor, to his wife, and to a number of family friends who walk by on their way in for the service. The viewing is coming to an end.

"Have you said your goodbyes?" says grandma as she turns towards Papa, our arms still around each other, side by side.

"I'm good," I say as I look at her. "I still have the book to finish. We're not done yet. Papa and I still have a lot left to do."

Grandma looks at me, then back at Papa. "He'll never leave you," she says.

If only that were true.

Then I wouldn't be writing this.

"Taps" is the saddest piece of music ever written.

I never would have said that before now. I know what it means in movies, but it's never meant anything to me personally, aside from being a sad sounding song. But once you truly experience it as a piece of a loss, you'll know. For every military family out there that's lost some one, I finally know.

The service began with Papa's blood relatives in the front row of pews. This consisted of me, my brother, my cousin Megan, my mom, and my grandma. The row behind us was for extended family, including my dad, my cousin's aunt, and Nicole, who sat directly behind me.

I flipped through the pamphlet that described the service. I saw that "Taps" was to be played at the very end. I knew then and there that any composure I had would be lost during that song.

The service was fine as far as those things go. The eulogy by the pastor involved Papa's military service. It was clear that the pastor had known Papa and before he began talking he was visibly upset. But I would think that anyone who'd ever had any kind of contact with Papa would be upset. He was larger than life. You couldn't help but be infected by Papa's good nature. He was so in love with life that you couldn't help but share in that feeling.

There was a hymn, "Eternal Father, Strong to Save." During the song they folded up the veil that had been lying on Papa's casket. They brought out an American flag. They unfolded it. They laid it on top of his casket.

The hymn ended. And from the back of the church came a trumpet.

I held my hand up to my face. My eyes filled with tears. A single drop fell down my cheek.

My family followed the casket out of the church. In the antechamber the pastor asked me if I wanted to help carry the casket into the hearse. I grabbed one end and helped carry Papa down the stairs, out the door, and into the car.

And that was it.

I never did say goodbye.

I don't know if I can.

PART TWO

How Did I Get Here?

10

What Do I Do Now?

I NEVER REALLY CRIED.

During "Taps" tears began to flow, but it was just for those few measures, and even then they were contained. But I never broke down, not like I knew I would later when I was alone.

Grieving is perhaps the most uniquely personal thing a human being can do. A room full of people can all grieve for the same reason, but none of them will grieve in the same way. Grief is specific to the person in a way that perhaps nothing else is. No one can ever truly understand how another person grieves; there are simply too many nuances to it. Between the outer projection of grief and the maelstrom of thoughts and feelings that fill the inside, no one can ever truly know what a person goes through when they're grieving. Psychiatrists can break down steps for grief all they want, but the specifics, the details of those steps are known only to that person.

I didn't cry in Ohio because I knew I would cry a lot in California. And I was right.

It's been almost a week since Papa's funeral. Because of a vacation Bible school at the church, the service was pushed back to two o'clock, with the viewing an hour earlier. Because of frustrating airline policies, Nicole and

I had no choice but to fly back to Los Angeles from our original airport of choice, in this case Cleveland. This meant we had a four hour drive waiting for us before our five hour plane ride.

These things added up to us missing the burial, as we had to leave directly after the service. I missed the Color Guard. I wasn't there to put an arm around my mom or hold my grandmother's hand as they lowered my grandfather into the ground. I don't even know what his tombstone looks like.

And now I'm back in Los Angeles and I have to try to make some kind of sense out of all of this.

We arrived back at the apartment just after midnight on Monday, July 10th. Tuesday night I sat down with a glass of whiskey and water and wrote about the events leading up to finding out Papa had died. Wednesday night I sat down with a glass of whiskey and water and wrote about everything that happened after that.

I cried more Wednesday night than I have in a very long time.

I downloaded "Taps" because I'm a sadist and because I need it to feel real.

I cried a lot. I cried when I wrote it, I cried afterwards, and I cried still later when I talked to Nicole. It's been a week since his funeral and there are still times when I feel like crying and I'm at the point now where I wonder when that's going to go away.

A common question posed to me since Papa's death was what I'm going to do with the book. The abstract answer is that I'm going to finish it; it's more important than ever.

I'm working on the specifics.

Papa's death has caused me to re-think this book, not so much if I'll finish, but how I go to this point. It had taken me a long time—far longer than I'd like to admit—to get to the point where I actually sat down to work on this book. And while I am absolutely sick over the fact that I didn't start it sooner, I'm also grateful that I was able to write any of it at all while Papa was still here. I feel like the fact that he knew I was writing it might have brought him some comfort when he was sick; I hope he had an understanding that his story would live on.

I didn't get to this point alone. I never would have made it this far by myself. I never would have gotten here without Nicole.

I spent most of 2004 completely alone. I had been living in Los Angeles for two years and I finally felt comfortable. I'd done all the usual West Coast things: Hollywood clubs, bad relationships, drunken debauchery, and nights that never ended. But none of that was me, and in 2004 I knew that. I was happy to just be by myself, to concentrate on the things that mattered most to me. In a lot of ways this was the year where I would really grow into myself. I became more confident not only in who I was, but in my writing ability.

And that was the rub, really: part of me was always afraid that I could never do my grandfather's life justice on the printed page. It's daunting; tell me how you write a book about a man who's done so much, who's meant so much to so many people? How was I supposed to write about a sixty year love affair when I'd never spent two years with the same girl? I have nearly as little knowledge about love as I do about war.

My entire family is going to read this. Marine Corps and Army buddies who have known my grandfather twice as long as I've been alive are going to read this. And, to be incredibly selfish, this could make or break my potential career as a writer.

By the end of 2004 the folder I'd set aside for research on my grandfather's life contained three letters, three photos, and two newspaper clippings. These things do not a book make.

But I still had the tapes my grandmother had sent me. In a small box on a shelf in my closet, sat two audio tapes filled with information and I barely looked at them, let alone listened to them. They'd now been in my possession for over a year and all they were doing was collecting dust.

Maybe subconsciously I was envisioning a book cover emblazoned with "Years in the Making."

Six years of college and two degrees kept convincing me that a book like this was too pedestrian for my big brain and maybe they were right. But ultimately this isn't a book about brains; it's a book about heart. And for whatever reason mine didn't seem to be getting the work out it needed to sit down and write. I knew how to use my head. My heart, however, was somewhat out of practice.

Then I met Nicole.

Aside from being raised around strong women, I was also raised by men who knew how to treat them. My most direct example of this was, of course, my dad, who more or less believed he'd be dead or worse if it weren't for my mom. He probably wouldn't phrase it that way, but he always gave the impression that he knew how lucky he was and that my mom meant more to him than pretty much anything else on the face of the earth. My dad never seemed to take my mom for granted and it seemed like he was always thinking about her. I can't count the number of times he'd show up after work with some surprise gift for her. It seemed like he spent all day thinking about what to get her.

My grandfather was much the same way and I think this was one of the few things Dad and Papa actually saw eye to eye on. Papa was always extremely thoughtful when it came to grandma. The fact that he was able to find the time to send her letters during WWII is perhaps the greatest example of this. But I only knew him after he'd retired, and my earliest memories are of my grandparents singing totally random and completely silly songs to each other.

That was how I was raised: strong women are good and respecting them is essential, so to say that I'd been prepared my entire life to meet Nicole wouldn't be an exaggeration.

Nicole and I met online, as staggeringly modern day as marrying someone you dated in high school seems old fashioned. Our relationship, like my grandparents', began through letters. We would e-mail each other for six weeks before ever meeting in person, laying the groundwork for what was to come one written word at a time.

When we finally met, we knew we would get along; it was just a matter of finding out if there was a spark or not. Then we had all the time in the world to explore that spark, since I wasn't preparing for an invasion of a hostile nation. And yet, there was still some sense of urgency, a similar whirlwind of romance; Nicole moved in with me just eight months after we met.

Nicole and I met, in person, on December 1, 2004, and even though we'd only been dating for a few weeks, it would still be hard for me to leave her when I went back to Ohio for Christmas.

I normally did my Christmas shopping when I got home on the 23rd, so I wouldn't have to take gifts with me on the flight back home. That year, however, there was a horrible snowstorm, and I wasn't able to go anywhere. I had to order gifts for my family online, but none of them would arrive in time for Christmas.

I can remember, on Christmas Eve, telling my mom that I would give her a gift to tide her over. I told her that I'd met a girl named Nicole, but that we'd only been dating for a month, and that I would probably be up late talking to her on the phone, since she was with her family in the California.

It was Christmas in abstract; I gave my mom Nicole, and hope for another daughter in-law. Papa would give me the title of this book.

We'd all sat down for dinner—my parents, my brother and his wife, my nephews, my grandparents, and me—and my grandmother said grace, as she does every year. I suppose that's another indication of the matriarchy that is my family.

As soon as my grandmother said "Amen," as soon as everyone repeated her, as soon as everyone looked up at each other and at the food in front of us, my grandfather said these words:

"I pray hardest when I'm being shot at."

And everyone laughed.

"Papa, that's what I'm calling the book," I said.

He meant it as a joke, but it was so much more. It summarized a big part of my grandfather in so many ways. It not only made reference to his military service through three wars, it was also a great indication on how he looked at life. My grandfather has always had a positive outlook, has always managed to see the best in things. He's always been a joyful person. It's sometimes easier to remember the sound of his laugh than his voice.

At the same time, I can picture Papa, years younger, in the middle of Vietnam or the mountains of Korea or high above the South Pacific, squeezing his hands together as hard as he could, looking upwards, gritting his teeth, and whispering various pleas to God as he prepared himself for yet another battle.

I'm still astounded that not only was he able to make that joke, but with the realization that it was a joke based in real life: my grandfather had been shot at, most likely on more than one occasion. I could only imagine how many times he'd come close to dying.

I had a title. I still had no book.

The funny thing about being in love is how it suddenly usurps everything else in your life. My grandfather was at war and he still found time to write letters to my grandmother. In times of life and death, all that mattered was love.

I spent the majority of 2005 just being in love. Nicole and I had our ups and downs, of course, but all of that just seemed to make us stronger. For us, it was more than just the honeymoon period, it was the building period. We were creating a foundation upon which we planned to build something magnificent. No matter what, we always knew that this was real. It was the kind of blind faith that I'd never known before. For Nicole and I, there were obstacles, but nothing would stop us.

I think about my grandparents and everything they went through and I realize just how important those convictions are. Even divorce couldn't keep them apart; it was just another obstacle to overcome.

I flew home that July for my grandparents' 60th anniversary. The running joke was that there should have been an asterisk next to that "60," since they were counting from the date of their first marriage.

The local newspaper had asked area couples who had been married for more than fifty years to contribute to an article on what makes a good marriage. This was Grandma's contribution:

> *Remember:*
> *Your spouse is not as perfect as you*
> *Your "please and thank you's"*
> *Your spouse is not a mind reader*
> *Also:*
> *Find a faith you are both comfortable in*
> *Stand united when raising children*
> *Keep your differences between yourselves*
> *Never end the day without a kiss of love*
> *And of course, we all know how important it is to have a sense of humor*

It was amazing for me to read that, and to see just how many of them applied to Nicole and me.

The anniversary celebration had been great and I was glad I was able to make it home for it. My mom bought my plane ticket and my grandfather paid for the hotel room, so my contribution mostly consisted of showing up and drinking their whiskey.

At one point, towards the end of the night when most of the guests had headed home, I noticed that my grandfather's drink was almost gone. I offered to get him a fresh one, as I was in need of a new one myself.

"Papa," I said, "I think we could use a couple of drinks." My plan was to sit down with him over one of the few things we had in common: whiskey and water.

By the time I returned, however, it was time to wrangle my nephews to bed, so our meeting of the minds was going to have to wait. Oh, we still had our drinks, of course, we just shared them with my parents and my grandma as we watched my brother and his wife gather up their boys to go.

On the surface it would seem like this would have been the beginning of my foray into this book, that my attempt at some one on one time with grandfather was my first attempt at getting some information out of him. But that wasn't the case. My head was still elsewhere.

Nicole would help me with this, at first inadvertently, then intentionally.

From the end of July 2005 until the end of December 2005 I spent time with some or all of Nicole's family on five separate occasions. I had always known how much family had meant to her, but I didn't realize the extent.

I think this was another thing that was hard for me comprehend. I care about my family, of course, but it's not necessary for me to see them more than twice a year. But Nicole lists "proximity to family" near the top of her list of important considerations when choosing a place to live. I tend to think that living further away gives me more independence, but at a cost.

Nicole needs to see her family on a regular basis and it's easy to see why: she'd been taught at a very young age that family was important. And it became more and more clear to me that they wanted Nicole to end up with someone who felt the same way.

Fortunately, I had two things going for me: an astounding memory and a grandfather I planned on writing a book about.

My astounding memory allowed me to recite lengthy branches on Nicole's family tree at the drop of a hat. In many ways these people were going to be as important to me as Nicole; I have no doubts her parents would have accepted me into the family regardless, but knowing that I made a point of remembering names and dates and connections made me that much more appealing.

Then there was my grandfather. Nicole's dad, also a veteran, was particularly interested in Papa. I would mention small things in passing—really the only things I knew up until that point—and Nicole's dad seemed to consider my knowledge to be an indication that family was important to me.

But I felt as if I were something of an imposter, spreading bits and pieces about my grandfather without being able to back it up with more substantial information. I felt like I should have known more than I did, like I should have been able to tell lengthy stories that had been related to me over nightcaps.

In fact, it was becoming clear to me just how much of an influence my grandfather had been. If I were to ask any of Nicole's family members about my family, they'd probably be able to provide more information on my grandfather than on anyone else because I talked about him the most.

On top of that, in 2005 I spent my first Christmas away from Ohio. I'd spent every Christmas of my first twenty-nine years on this earth in Kent with my family, but this time I was going to spend the holidays with Nicole's family in California. My mom had made a point of calling me on a regular basis over the few days that normally marked my visit home. My absence was evidently taking a toll on her. I'll admit that it was hard for me, too, but I had recently turned thirty and viewed it as something of a rite of passage. I figured that at some point I was going to start a family of my own and then my parents were going to have to come to me.

That's another thing about falling in love: it makes you think crazy things.

To make matters worse for everyone involved, my grandfather had some heart trouble the day before he and my grandmother were to make the drive up from their home in Huber Heights to my parents' house in Kent. It hadn't been anything serious, but it was enough to keep them at their place for Christmas.

I had already planned on calling home on Christmas Day, but Papa's heart scare made me want to call sooner. So, on Christmas Eve, on the back porch of Nicole's aunt and uncle's house in Oakland, I called my grandparents in Ohio.

They both sounded good—positive and upbeat. The truly unfortunate thing was that I think this was the first time I'd ever called them from California, at least when my parents weren't there visiting as well. I can blame that on the e-mail machine we got them all I want, but the sad fact is that I'm not a fan of talking on the phone, even when it comes to my own family.

It was great to talk to them, though, and I mentioned to Papa that the book about him was still on my mind, that I was still going to use the title he'd given me a year earlier. He laughed and told me the phrase had just popped out, spur of the moment. I told him it was a keeper.

When we got off the phone he told me he and my grandmother loved me and I said it back. That's something of a rarity in my family and I suppose, looking back on it, it was another marker leading me towards the inevitable.

As we approached the end of the year, I made a list of projects I wanted to work on. This book was on that list, but there were still a few things ahead of it.

Nicole was about to change that.

On New Year's Eve, 2005, Nicole and I had dinner at the Stinking Rose. It's one of Nicole's favorite restaurants and we'd made it a point of trying to go there on a regular basis. It was just something nice we could do every once in a while, a reminder of those dates we used to go on after we'd first met.

We were going to a party after that, but ate kind of early, given the night, and had to kill some time at the bar. Not that this was a problem for us. Nicole and I have this incredible ability to have a great time doing absolutely nothing at all. And since we were taking cabs all night long, we were free to indulge in a few drinks.

At about 7:30 my cell phone rang. It was my parents.

I knew that my mom would call because she was probably feeling sentimental and they were at my grandparents' house, which I imagine only made that worse. We talked for a bit, I filled them in on what I was doing that night, and eventually exchanged a few "Happy New Year's" and that was that.

When I got off the phone, I explained to Nicole that they were at my grandparents' house.

The following is paraphrased from memory:

"You know," said Nicole, "you keep trying to get your foot in the door with an agent—I don't think anyone would pass up a book about your grandfather."

"Wow," I said, as I'd never really considered it before.

"What agent or publisher wouldn't see how easy it would be to sell that?"

"No joke," I said. "The biography of a three-war veteran, the story of a sixty-two-year love affair, would be a best seller—I'd be on Oprah's book club for sure."

"So why don't you write it?"

And there it was.

Why don't I write it?

11

The 174th

THE DAY OF PAPA'S FUNERAL, MY GRANDMA didn't just give me his discharge form, she also gave me some more pictures, the latest issue of The VHPA Aviator (the newsletter for the Vietnam Helicopter Pilots Association), and a few names and addresses of people Papa had served with. Grandma only had a few, but knew that Papa had kept in contact with them, if not often than at least regularly. She also told me that they were in Vietnam with him, and that she didn't know of anyone he'd served with in Korea.

I honestly had no idea what I was in for. I didn't know how much digging I'd have to do to find information on Papa's days in either Korea or Vietnam. I had visions of being on hold with the Army as I tried to find the names of people Papa served with. The extent of my information at the moment was a photocopy of a letter detailing his military career that Papa had sent to an Army buddy who was writing a book about Vietnam, and I had no idea how to get a hold of that guy.

On Friday, July 14, I decided to fire the opening salvo of the next part of the book. The first part was my grandfather telling me about his life. Since he was no longer here, the second half would have to be his life through other people's eyes.

I had no idea what to expect. I certainly wasn't expecting Lt. Col. Bernie Cobb (Ret.) and the men of the 174th Assault Helicopter Company (AHC).

Lt. Col. Cobb was one of the first names my grandmother gave me and it was one that I recognized. I knew I'd seen a picture of him and Papa in Vietnam together and I was pretty sure he'd been mentioned in a letter I read somewhere. At this point my folder for information on Papa was pretty thick. If I were better organized I'm sure I'd have a spreadsheet.

I called Mr. Cobb on Friday afternoon. His wife answered the phone:

"Can I talk to Bernie Cobb, please?" I said.

"Who's calling?" she said.

"Um, Robert Stuart's grandson." I hadn't given this much thought, actually. He wasn't going to know my name from Adam. It was strange to be using my grandfather's name like that.

"Bernie!" I heard her call out. "Robert Stuart's grandson is on the phone!" She said it with a certain level of enthusiasm, as if she either knew Papa personally or knew of him, but that either way he had left a good impression.

I don't know if he thought it at the time, but such a phone call could not have filled Mr. Cobb's mind with good thoughts.

I introduced myself and I told him that my grandfather had died. He told me he was sorry to hear that. "I just talked to him a few weeks ago," he said.

This is a comment I would get a lot as I began researching. It seems that after his heart valve replacement surgery, Papa had called a lot of his old Army buddies. Perhaps it was his way of doing some housekeeping, of leaving that one last good impression. Each person told me he sounded just like he always did and acted as if nothing was wrong. I have no doubts that that's exactly what Papa wanted them to believe. He wanted to be remembered the way he'd led his life, not as a sickly person in a hospital bed.

I told Mr. Cobb that I was writing a book about Papa and that if he could help me, I would really appreciate it. I told him that my grandmother had mentioned that Mr. Cobb was a big fan of e-mail, and that perhaps it would be an easier and more efficient to communicate.

Mr. Cobb asked for my grandmother's address so he and his wife could send along their condolences. I told him I'd include that in the e-mail as I didn't have it on me.

As soon as that call ended, I called my grandmother. I'd planned on doing so this week, anyway, and this way I could tell her that I'd talked to Mr. Cobb.

My grandmother sounded good and seemed happy with the fact that I'd begun contacting people. She thanked me for staying for the funeral and told me to thank Nicole for staying. She told me that Papa would have been so happy to see everyone together. I could hear her beginning to cry and she passed the phone to my cousin.

A few minutes later I was firing off my first e-mail to Lt. Col. Cobb. I had a feeling he'd be a useful source for information on Vietnam.

I had no idea what I was in for.

The 174th Assault Helicopter Company has its own web site. I'm pretty confident that it will still be there if and when this book gets published because the people who have put it together are dedicated to one thing: making sure that the men who served in the 174th AHC are not forgotten.

Aside from giving him grandma's address, my initial e-mail to Mr. Cobb was simply a "thank you" for agreeing to help me fill some blanks over the coming weeks. He wrote me back three hours later and copied a number of other people on the response.

He gave me some background on how he met my grandfather. He also told me that he had copied the two men who ran the 174th AHC web site on the e-mail, and that one of the men also ran the 174th's e-mail list.

In the span of the next two hours I got two more e-mails from Mr. Cobb, the first a copy of what he'd sent in to the 174th mailing list, the second a forward of the e-mail he'd received from the list, which announced to the group (310 in all) that Papa had passed on.

He was described as a "true hero" and a "patriot." They said he was one of a kind.

Getting that e-mail did me in for a bit. I forwarded it to my parents and my brother. I almost copied my grandma on it, but decided it would be better to mail it to her, as perhaps reading it on the tiny e-mail machine we got her would be frustrating somehow.

I was impatient, so I called home to see if my parents had checked their e-mail.

My dad answered the phone. He said that my mom was taking a bath, so he filled me in on what had happened since I left Ohio.

"Did you hear about the bank teller?" he said, and this must have been proof of his psychic powers because my grandma had actually mentioned something about a bank teller to me when I'd called.

"Yeah, Grandma mentioned something when I called her," I said.

It turns out that my parents and my grandma sold one of my grandparents' cars. They had sold it for cash to a man who'd done all the maintenance on the car over the years. The man knew Papa and made them a good offer, in no small part because he liked and respected my grandfather.

That leads us to the bank teller. Besides needing to deposit the some three thousand dollars in cash they were carrying, my parents and my grandma needed to consolidate some accounts. So they went to the bank to do so. And even there my grandfather's legacy was apparent.

"He was visibly upset," said my dad, describing how the bank teller reacted when they explained to him that Papa had died. He knew Papa from the times that he came in to do his banking. And those times that they'd interacted had left an impression on him.

The *Dayton Daily News* posts their obituaries on their web sites. There's a guest book for each entry and the bank teller actually wrote a comment: "...we will miss his smiling face and infectious laugh."

There was the epitome of my grandfather, in one single day. It was e-mails from brothers in arms. It was the mechanic who probably saw him twice a year. It was the bank teller, who my parents said looked to be just about my age.

He touched everyone who met him.

And, I'm hoping, even those who didn't.

It's been a month and a day since Papa died.

My grandmother set aside a few things for me she thought I might like. There was an envelope full of pictures. There was the tape recorder I'd sent them years ago, as well as the remaining blank tapes. And there was a note pad. Only one page had been written on. It was the beginning of the letter that Papa was working on when he died. It's dated March and this is what it says:

> *Hi Kyle,*
>
> *Time to get to our fearless saga! One event I forgot to mention that your grandmother says you may find of interest. Along about Sept. of 1944 our crew received five days "rest and recuperation": leave in Sidney, Australia. That is, five days IN Sidney, travel time there was extra!!*

That was all he wrote in March. The next section is from the end of April:

> *Quite some jump there, eh? By now you know the reason why. What a revolting development and certainly the most unexpected. Who would of expected open heart surgery. A "valve job" so to speak. I'm not writing too well yet. I'm in re-hab at Maria Joseph Rehab Center in Dayton. It used to be a Catholic rest home, but is now into physical re-hab, any brand. I hope to get to go home early next week. I'm ready right now but first you have to cross all the "T's". Megan was here from Vermont for a week, goes home Friday. Your mother was down for nearly a week.*

And that was it. That was the end of the last letter he would ever write me. Just over two months later he'd no longer be here.

It's that last letter that's motivating me today. It's that last letter that's moving me forward, that's telling me it's time to get back to it, that's pointing at the Korean War and telling me that I need to pick up where I left off.

While I knew Mr. Cobb and the men of the 174th would be incredibly helpful when I started the section on Papa's time in Vietnam, it seemed like I was going to be flying blind when it came to Korea. Even my grandmother had no idea how to get in touch with anyone Papa served with then. Papa had been to Marine Corps reunions for WWII and the 174th had a reunion in Florida every year. But Papa didn't do anything like that for Korea.

The same day that the message went out to the 174th that Papa had died, I got an e-mail from one of their number, a man named Bob Jones. I don't know what the percentages on this are, particularly considering how big the American military is, but Mr. Jones explained to me that he had actually served with my grandfather twice, the first time being in Korea. Not only was this man still around, not only was he active on the computer, but he served with Papa twice with a break in between of over a decade.

I suppose I should call that good luck, but the fact that I'm writing the remainder of the book without Papa undermines any claims to "good" luck I might make.

Papa only briefly covers his time in Korea in the letter he sent me: "As the Korean conflict ground down, went off to fly O-1's with the second field artillery group, that was corps artillery for the second ROK corps in the mountains of central Korea, several clicks north of the reservoir there."

This would have been directly following the end of the war, when the Korean Demilitarized Zone was officially established. This would also be the time when United Nation forces would transfer those front line defenses to the South Koreans.

Robert Stuart, Warren, Ohio (date unknown).

My greatgrandfather, Seth Stuart, during his time with the U.S. 13th Cavalry, circa 1916.

My grandfather, Robert Stuart, age 16.

Robert Stuart, Perris Island, South Carolina, 1942.

Robert Stuart, age 20. Australia, 1944.

Emirau Island, Papua New Guinea, 1944. Standing (*left to right*):
Eugene Henry, navigator; Lt. Ray Smith, pilot; Lt. Hugh Price,
co-pilot. Front (*left to right*): Don Keefe, aerial gunner; Robert
Stuart, radio gunner; David Cosby, aerial gunner.

Elizabeth Anne Davis, my grandmother. Warren, Ohio.

Anne Davis (*left*) with Robert and his sister, Betty. Warren, Ohio, 1945.

Robert and Anne, Feb. 1945.

Robert Stuart and Sherry-Beth Stuart, my mom, at 5 months. Case Western University, Cleveland, Ohio, 1946.

Goldie Stuart, my great-grandmother, Robert and Sherry-Beth. Warren, Ohio, 1951.

Robert in Qui Nhon, Vietnam, 1966.

Front (*left to right*): Maj. Bernie Cobb, Maj. Robert Stuart. Back (*left to right*): Maj. Walt Payne, Maj. Jim Shrader. Qui Nhon, Vietnam, 1966.

(*Left to right*): Maj. Mel Tate, Maj. Bernie Cobb, Maj. Robert Stuart. Qui Nhon, Vietnam, 1966.

Members of the 174th Assualt Helicopter Command (*left to right*): Maj. Dick
Legener, unknown, Maj. Harry Rober (48th Aviation Company), Chief
Warrant Officer Bob Gauthier, Maj. Robert Stuart. Vietnam, 1966.

Robert (*left*) at Fort Knox, Kentucky. Circa 1967.

Kyle Garret, "Bridget" and Robert Stuart. Summer 1980.

Papa and me, May 2004.

Since this letter was a copy of a letter Papa sent to someone he'd served with in Vietnam, he mentions that he flew in O-1's, which is what they were designated by the time Vietnam came around, In Korea, however, they were known as L-19's, or the Cessna "Bird Dog." The main appeal of these planes was that they could take off and land in relatively small areas. They only carried two people, but they were ideal for small cargo drops, reconnaissance, and even medical evacuation for a single person.

However, it had one main drawback: it lacked armor.

I can't help but think about my grandfather's WWII duties and how he'd moved from placing himself in one ridiculously dangerous situation to another one. The war might have been over, but Papa was flying through the newly formed DMZ in a small plane with no armor. On top of that, it wasn't a particularly fast plane, either. A single enemy soldier with a rifle could take the "Bird Dog" out of the sky.

The scale of this was hard for me to understand, until I learned that North and South Korea still shoot at each other from opposite sides of the DMZ. While North Korea might make the news for other reasons, a few shots at each other never get much press. It's never a lot of shooting, but it has happened often enough in the past sixty years for it to be routine.

"Winter of '53-'54," wrote Papa, "snow up our eyeballs and so cold we kept breaking the tail wheel springs." While my knowledge of aviation may be limited, breaking tail wheel springs doesn't sound like a good thing.

"Living in double layer tents with fuel oil stoves," he wrote. "Very scenic."

The "very scenic" line is so typical of my grandfather. It was hard to imagine that he was able to appreciate the scenery during a war, yet I know that he would have. If he were still alive, I'd ask him about it, and he'd make a joke, and he'd laugh and pat me on the knee. I don't think I'll ever forget his laugh.

"As the DMZ was established," he continued, "the II Corps group was turned over to the Koreans and we all went elsewhere. I went to I Corps artillery in the west side of the country."

Fortunately for me, Papa didn't just move from one section of Korea to another, he moved somewhere that left a trail, a tangible thread remaining even after he'd gone, that I stumbled upon without even looking.

I sent Bob Jones an e-mail in hopes that he might be able to shed some light on the second half of Papa's time in the DMZ.

The I Corps Artillery Aviation was based at an airfield named A-160, although exactly what that stood for I'm not sure. It was just below the 38th Parallel, the famous division between the two Koreas, and next to a number of strangely named mountains, including Alligator Jaws, Crazy Horse, Pork Chop Hill, and the Dagmars.

Pork Chop Hill was the sight of two major battles during the war, the last coming just weeks before the armistice. Both U.N. and Communist Chinese Forces took heavy casualties. While it was originally held by the U.N. forces, it was later claimed by the CCF. Nearly 350 U.S. soldiers were killed in the two battles, and over a thousand were wounded.

Papa was stationed in the shadow of those who had died for their country. Knowing my grandfather, I can picture him looking out onto Pork Chop Hill every morning and using it as inspiration for the day ahead.

The airfield was made of crushed rock. The runway wasn't much wider than the space from one landing gear to the other and the taxi ways were even smaller. This left little margin for error, and even that little margin was taken away by the steep drop off into a river on one end of the runway. In other words, only the best pilots were making runs out of this airfield.

Evidently, the Korean pilots were less than thrilled with the layout. The U.S. pilots, however, actually enjoyed it. I suppose there could be an argument made as to the gung-ho nature of the American military, the cavaliering John Wayne attitude that's probably much less prominent in other cultures. There's also probably a decent argument to be made about how much more intensely the American military trains, particularly leading up to the first major conflict of the Cold War.

According to Mr. Jones, they flew the "Bird Dog" for most of the time, although later started using the L-20 "Beaver" plane, appropriately enough built by the Canadians. Mr. Jones called it a better plane and I'm willing to take his word for it. Their missions were mostly artillery adjustment, again working to establish the DMZ.

It's sad to say, but up until this point the extent of my knowledge of the Korean War probably came from watching M.A.S.H. re-runs. Surprisingly enough, it seemed like Mr. Jones had a feeling that this was the case. I suppose in a lot of ways Korea is the war that people forget, as it lacked the scale of WWII and the contention of Vietnam.

Regardless, pop culture was about to be validated, at least on some level.

Mr. Jones wrote: "We lived in General Purpose 'GP' Medium tents for most of our stay in Korea. I think we had six officers to a tent with folding cots lining the sides of the tent. A small diesel fueled stove provided the heat and nothing provided air conditioning other than raise the tent flaps. Watch M.A.S.H. and the doctors that lived in 'The Swamp,' as they called their tent, lived as we did."

While this might have been an accurate depiction, this also served to fill my head with images of my grandfather drinking homemade liquor out of giant martini glasses. I'm sure I could easily prove that image wrong, but it's not necessary and, really, it's somewhat soothing.

Since my grandfather and Mr. Jones were lieutenants, they had access to the officers' club, which was basically two tents joined together. For a while they had to go through the mess hall lines with everyone else, until they actually brought on a few Korean boys from the area to work as runners to bring the officers food. The officers actually chipped in and bought china plates and good eating utensils. They even had a small bar built in the officers' club. As Mr. Jones said in his e-mail, "Living good! At least for those times."

Papa would end his tour in Korea in October of 1954, twenty-one years to the month before I would be born.

This is something I can never understand, from an e-mail from Mr. Jones: "I don't remember the unit that Bob [my grandfather] was assigned to at the time or when he joined us. I do remember Bob very well. We all became close there, as could be expected."

I will never be able to understand the comradery these men had. I will never be able to understand what they went through, whether it was WWII, Korea, or Vietnam. I can't imagine trusting someone with your life, placing yourself in someone else's hands. We don't remember what it was like to be a baby, to be dependent upon our mothers for life. But in essence that's what these men were doing. Faltering in your duties could mean death not just for you, but for those serving with you.

In the same e-mail Mr. Jones mentions that he has pictures of my grandfather that he will scan and send to me once he's able to sort through some boxes. He's just had hip replacement surgery and he's moving very slowly. He also mentions that he'd just spoken to my grandfather a month earlier. Papa had called him when he'd started having his health problems.

They're all growing old. My grandfather called both Bob Jones and Bernie Cobb when his health problems began, perhaps in an effort to prepare for the worst, or maybe to convince himself that everything would be okay. Maybe he thought talking to them would trigger something deep down, some reserve of vitality that he'd called upon whenever he was sent on another mission. Or perhaps he just wanted to make sure that he was able to talk to these people one last time before he left us.

My dad pointed something out to me. Papa didn't die in a hospital. He died in the car, leaving the hospital and heading home. And while he might not have gotten where he wanted to go, he did escape.

Even when he was at his worst, when he was near death and the only option was to have the heart valve replacement surgery, he still wanted to go home. I think it was instinctive: after the life he'd lead, he didn't want his final moments to come lying on a bed surrounded by doctors.

He'd spent his life doing great things. He'd spent his life on foreign soil, putting himself in danger, tempting fate time and again. In many ways it would seem inappropriate for him to die slowly, to fade away while lying in a hospital.

He got out, even if he never made it home.

12

Paradise…and Snakes

IN HER MEMOIRS, MY GRANDMOTHER SAYS IT was "husbands and wives reunited in paradise."

Hawaii has always been a special place to my family. My earliest memories involve the Hawaiian artwork in my grandparents' house, cans of Macadamia nuts in our pantry—hand delivered by my grandparents—and an endless stream of photos and videos of island vacations. My grandparents would go back often, more often than I could keep track. It was really hard on Papa when he became too old to manage the long flight out to the Pacific. Going to Hawaii was important to my grandparents, which made it important to my entire family, made it magical. And yet I've never set foot there, even thought I currently live so close.

A few years ago my grandparents took my parents to Hawaii and since then my parents have made it a point of going almost every year. It's worked out well on two fronts, as they also get to spend a few days on their way back in Los Angeles visiting their wayward son.

Being a boy in Ohio, Hawaii seemed like another world.

Papa puts it like this: "As the war had ended the Army decided to withdraw the 25th Infantry Division out of Korea and return it to its base at Schofield Barracks in Hawaii. I took an 'inter-theater' transfer and caught the fourth (and last) transport ferrying the 25th to Hawaii. That was a really great 'fun' tour."

Grandma and my mom drove to San Francisco from Ohio and were put up in Ft. Mason en route to Hawaii. On November 29, 1954, they boarded the General Sultan and set sail to meet up with my grandfather.

It's interesting to note the difference between war time and peace time. While my grandfather only gives the barest of details on his time spent in Hawaii (albeit in a letter to an Army buddy), my grandmother covers a good amount of ground on their time there. I suppose being stationed in Hawaii is less a military move and more a domestic one.

"Had a fun bunch of pilots in the air section," wrote Papa, "and even though we were all assigned to different regiments and div HDQ we operated as a 'company.' CO, XO, OPS, etc. each unit had an H-13 and an O-1, plus two U-6's at Div."

While Papa mentions the "Birddog", he also mentions the H-13 Sioux, which was a helicopter. Up until this point Papa had been flying planes. This was the first time he'd mentioned helicopters.

But that was it. That was the extent of what my grandfather said about Hawaii.

It's that negative space that makes this hard. The letter I'm using wasn't even written to me. On top of that, it was written for the expressed purpose of giving a point by point detail of Papa's military career, in theory back story for a book that a man who'd served under Papa was writing. And while I know the military was important to Papa, I know that it wasn't everything. I know that his family was more important. But I'll never have the chance to hear any of that from him, at least with regards to his tour of duty in paradise.

Fortunately, my grandmother wasn't about to just breeze over what was perhaps the best few years of her life, or at least the best place she ever lived.

It took my mom and my grandma five days to get to Hawaii by boat, finally reuniting with my grandfather on December 4, 1954, just three days shy of Pearl Harbor Day.

"We sailed on the *General Sultan* on November 29th and it took five days and nights," wrote Grandma in her memoirs. "Some storms made it rough at one point and everything in the room was tied down. In the dining room, the table cloths were wet down so the dishes wouldn't slide. There were four bunks in the room we had and a bath between two rooms. Sherry had some queasy time, but we fared pretty well. The night before we docked, the ship dropped anchor off shore. The lights of Honolulu were lovely."

The perks of island living were not lost on my grandmother: "It was great waking up to sunshine every day. Even when there were showers, they soon passed and the sun returned. We went to the Ft. De Russey beach on Christmas Day, so we could brag on it. However in February a Kona Storm came and it rained for days."

The following April, my mom turned nine and my grandparents got her a dog. They named the dog "Frisky."

I think I mentioned before that my grandma has an incredible memory. She even goes a step further in proving just how much she recalls from that time: "For Sherry's ninth birthday, April 17, 1955, Stu found a little black puppy for her. She named him "Frisky" and he really was. The problem was not with him, it was with our lack of knowledge about dog training. He would have been a better pet if we'd have house trained him and had him neutered. As it was, he had a dog house and when his male hormones raged, he'd break loose and get picked up by the Military Police. We would bail him out for 50¢."

That same year Papa was named Captain of the 27th Infantry and was, yet again, profiled in the local Warren, Ohio paper: "Stuart Promoted

To Capt. In Army." Papa's former classmates must have been sick of reading about him in the paper all the time.

While my grandparents and my mom hold a special place in their hearts for Hawaii, no one could claim a deeper connection with the islands than my uncle: He was born there. Grandma mentions in her memoirs that she became pregnant in the spring of '56; my Uncle Rob was born on February 13, 1957.

My grandma said that Uncle Rob was four weeks late and was a long, difficult birth. His birth would be something of a premonition of things to come. My uncle would not have an easy or long life and there's a certain amount of cruel irony to be found in the fact that a man with so many inner demons would be born in a virtual paradise.

While some children might see a new sibling as a threat to what makes them unique, my mom was not one of them. "Sherry was so excited to finally have a little brother," wrote Grandma, "and she was such a help with his care. If we had a sitter, she wouldn't let the sitter do anything. So after she turned eleven in April, we began to trust her 'sitting' for short periods. Being on a military reservation, security was good, and we usually were somewhere on post."

But while my uncle might have been able to claim Hawaii as his place of origin, he certainly couldn't claim to have any memories from those days. Just four months after my uncle was born, Papa got his next assignment, and the family headed stateside.

The time spent in the town of Enterprise, Alabama is one that gets referenced a lot in my family. My grandparents finally bought their first house there, with three bedrooms, one and a half bathrooms and a large yard. They even had two horses, which is actually why their stay gets brought up in conversation. My family has always been suburban, so it's hard for me to imagine my mom riding horses. She also had her first run in with a poisonous snake in the barn that held those horses, a run in that would prove to be the tip of the iceberg for my mom and snakes.

During their time there, it actually snowed in Enterprise, something that only happens once every fifty years or so.

Snake notwithstanding, Enterprise seemed like a slice of domestic bliss, between the house and the horses. It didn't last long, though, as Papa was again on the move and Grandma was left to take care of two children on her own.

Papa was sent to Fort Walters in Texas for helicopter training, or as my grandfather refers to it in his letter, "that rotary wing course."

"We all knew, and worked on, concepts of and became the air mobile Army, with rotary wings as the backbone," he wrote. The "rotary wings" were helicopters, different from the stationary wings of a plane. This had to have been a pretty big change for Papa, as it's clear to even a layman like myself that flying a helicopter would require a different set of skills than flying a plane.

It's also clear that Papa learned quickly, as in a few years time he'd be asked to head the 174th AHC for a tour of duty in Vietnam.

But that was still years off. In the meantime, my mom's run in with that one poisonous snake in Alabama was going to look like a walk in the park compared to what came next: life in Taiwan.

It's the little things that make this difficult.

Re-reading the first part of this book has been difficult. Re-reading it for typos and coming across lines written while Papa was still here is hard. I would imagine the editing process is going to be even worse.

I got a new cell phone recently. I had to put all of the phone numbers from my old phone into the new one. The listing that used to say "Grandparents" now simply says "Grandma."

It's the little things that you never see coming.

I remember a particular story from my childhood. The story, as it went, involved orientation in Taiwan. It also involved a bag full of snakes. It involved a bag of poisonous snakes, to be specific.

In the story, the Army held an orientation for Americans who had recently arrived in Taiwan, a country with an overabundance of poisonous snakes. In a lecture hall, a snake handler brought out a bag full of every kind of snake found on the island and dumped them on to the floor. These snakes were all very much alive.

The orientation class consisted of the snake handler, standing in the middle of floor covered with poisonous snakes, pointing out each type of snake to the Americans in the class and explaining to them their habits, where they were commonly found, and what to do if bitten by one.

For my entire life I'd always attributed that story to my mom, assuming that the lecture had been for families who were meeting enlisted men in Taiwan. I think I also attributed it to my mom because she'd been pretty vocal about her fear of snakes. She said that when walking back to her house in Taipei she could actually hear snakes slithering around on the ground around her, be it under rice patties or just to the edges of the road. I figured that a room full of snakes was probably the Army's way of scaring some respect into the kids who traveled there with their parents.

But I asked her about it the other day and she doesn't remember anything like that. She mentioned again walking through parts of town and hearing the snakes in the distance, but she has no memory of being in a room with a snake handler and a bag of snakes.

When she told me that, it was as if an imaginary block had been lifted, and I suddenly remembered the exact moment I heard that story. It was Papa who had told me about it. I was sitting on the living room floor in my grandparents' house. He was sitting in the rocking chair. I don't remember how the subject came up, but he was the one who told the story.

Since I am, in fact, scared of snakes, the gist of the story stuck with me through the years, even if the details didn't. Actually, now that I think about it, it might be the reason I'm scared of snakes.

"In 1960 got an assignment with the advisory group on Taiwan," wrote Papa in a letter to an old Army buddy. This was to be his first non-combat assignment in a foreign country. He'd spend six weeks prior to the trip at Arlington, Virginia, taking courses on Taiwan and diplomacy.

My grandparents, my mom, and my uncle arrived in Taiwan on November 29, 1960. Papa was stationed in Taipei.

As always, my grandma supplied me with the domestic details. They had their own house and two local women who would come to their house every day; one for household chores, the other to baby sit my uncle. It's interesting to think of how much exposure to people of different cultures my mom and her brother had while growing up. I've never known either of them to have a prejudiced bone in their bodies, and I think their experiences around the world played a big part in that.

Taiwan was a hot button issue. It was claimed by both the People's Republic of China, the Communist country who had sent troops into North Korea, and the Republic of China, who no longer had any control over mainland China and had tenuous control over the islands off the coast. Since Taipei was the capital of the Republic of China, the U.S. would take any opportunity to support non-Communist influence in that region, particularly as the Cold War continued to grow.

"Taiwan was a great tour," wrote Papa. "We had a couple of U-6's that we jumped both the team and their Chinese counterparts out of. My 'official' counterpart was a Chinese Major General named Chen, who was Chief of the Chinese Army Aviation."

Papa was not yet a major at this point, so it's particularly impressive that his "counterpart," as he says, was the Chief of Chinese Army Aviation. I can just picture Papa, Major General Chen, and two translators in a room talking about helicopters and decrying the mainland.

Papa and Major General Chen became such good compatriots that Chen was the one who pinned the "major's leaves" on Papa. It would seem that Papa was doing a pretty good job of establishing political ties with Taiwan for the U.S., ties that still hold nearly fifty years later.

Papa got yet more time in print, as his arrival in Taiwan was featured in *Niles Daily Times*, a local Warren, Ohio, newspaper that no longer exists. Grandma's dad and step-mother had shared a letter they'd received from their daughter with the local society columnist. Agnes Lopatta wrote "Town Talk" and the talk of the town in December of 1960 was the Stuart family.

The column is basically a verbatim retelling of the letter my grandmother sent her parents. She mentions the journey from San Francisco to Taiwan and that the weather changed drastically depending upon which island they stopped on to refuel. "We lost Thanksgiving Day along the way and gained eight hours," she wrote, "Friday was 32 hours long!"

"Our sponsors, Capt. and Mrs. Kendall met our plane," wrote Grandma, "along with Col. and Mrs. Murphy, who is the air section commanding officer. Sherry and I each received an orchid corsage and they brought us to the hotel, 'The Grand.' The hotel is owned by Madame Chiang and it's real plush."

Grandma goes on to describe their new three bedroom duplex, complete with coal burning hot water heater and room for the Amah, their live-in maid.

"The local scene," wrote Grandma, "is just like you see in travelogues, some parts fascinating, some parts pitiful. They utilize every inch for crops in Taiwan and work seven days a week. You see peddlers in the street with all kind of things—food, flowers, and coal."

The best part of the column, though, comes when the writer goes from simply quoting Grandma to relating what the letter said:

"There are some items where Anne has found a marked difference in cost and one in particular is the beauty shops in Taiwan. She and her daughter had their hair done in a shop, completely equipped with modern, up-to-date furnishings for only seventy-five cents each. How's that, gals?"

And with that my narrow view of the '60s was confirmed.

Everything seemed to be working out well for Papa. As he said in a letter, "Enjoyed our two years there and would have extended but our daughter who was a junior in Taipei American School wanted to come back to U.S. for her senior year in high school. Our son who turned five could care less one way or the other."

On May 15, 1962, Papa was made a major. He received his next assignment a few months later, and the family again found themselves returning to the States. After traveling and spending the holidays with family, they finally arrived at Ft. Devens in Massachusetts where Papa was to be the Corps Aviation Officer of the XIII Corps.

"A three hat job," wrote Papa, "Corps Aviation Officer, Corps Commander's personal pilot and supervisor to six college ROTC flight training programs in the Corps area."

More and more it seemed that Papa wasn't just being placed in a position to lead, but also in a position to teach, something that would become a theme in his life. Papa also mentions that he was on a first name basis with the Corps Commander: "He called me 'Bob' and I called him 'sir.'"

That line cracked me up the first time I read it.

That winter Papa built a makeshift ice rink in their backyard in Massachusetts for my uncle. They were definitely not in Taiwan anymore.

During this time Papa was also up for a promotion to lieutenant colonel. His superiors designated him "fully qualified but not selected," a result he would get multiple times over the course of his military career. No one could doubt Papa's performance, but some other factor was preventing him from being promoted.

My mom enrolled in the high school in Massachusetts halfway through her junior year so she was able to establish some kind of a life for herself before her senior year. She graduated in June of 1964 with honors, as my grandma points out in her memoirs. That fall she left for college at Kent State University, a somewhat ironic choice given what the future would hold for both my grandfather and Kent State. It was during her freshman year that my mom started driving from Kent to Warren, Ohio to visit Papa's mom, Goldie.

My mom wasn't going to be separated from her family for long, though. At the start of her sophomore year, my grandma and uncle moved yet again, choosing Kent to be their new home base, because Papa had gotten his orders for Vietnam.

13

Vietnam

THERE'S A WHITE ELEPHANT SITTING HERE next to me and I don't see that I have any choice but to address it. It's one of those things that I've spent all day avoiding simply because it's everywhere, to the extent that it no longer really holds the meaning that it should; it's simply become a way for people to get attention. I've been doing my best to avoid the subject all together, while to everyone else it's all they can talk about.

Today is September 11, 2006. It's the five-year anniversary of the largest foreign attack on the continental United States.

I didn't actually talk to my grandfather on that day. I talked to my dad, who told me that his mom mentioned how it reminded her of Pearl Harbor. My dad said that I would always remember where I was when I heard about the attack, the way that people in his generation remember where they were when they heard Kennedy had been assassinated. So my grandparents' generation had Pearl Harbor, my parents' generation had Kennedy, and I got the Twin Towers crashing to the ground, the result of an attack launched by an unseen enemy.

People react differently when I tell them what I'm working on. Not surprisingly, many people in Los Angeles instantly turn to the current war in Iraq. They want to know what my grandfather thought about it. I think many of them would consider any statement he'd make against the war to be vindication, as if their belief that the war is wrong would be validated by the opinions of a three war veteran and retired major.

Papa never commented on the righteousness of invading Iraq. I never heard him say a single word with regards to our motivations for going into that country. Now whether this was because he agreed with the decision or because he simply didn't believe a dissenting opinion really mattered, I don't know. If anything, Papa would have seen the machinations of those in power as secondary to the real issue: keeping the soldiers safe while they do their jobs to the best of their abilities.

Papa was not quiet about this point.

Get him talking, and Papa was very clear that he thought the war was being botched. This was particularly stunning considering both his personal history and his voting record. But Papa knew enough about war to know how it should be fought, and he was confused as to why it was being waged the way it was. I'm positive that he voted to re-elect those same people in power, but he held out hope that they would change the way they were operating in Iraq.

Papa could care less about those in charge; he cared about those who would have to do the dirty work. He cared about the person on the front line, and it's part of what made him such a successful leader.

In the fall of 1965, Papa headed to Ft. Benning in Georgia to get the 174th AHC formed and combat ready as quickly as possible.

I had to do a little detective work to decipher exactly what Papa meant in this part of the letter: "I stopped at career branch in the puzzle palace and was told I was a 'hard charger' and had stepped on somebody's toes."

The "puzzle palace" is the National Security Agency, headquarter in Ft. Meade, Maryland. Papa went to the top to find out about being passed up for promotion. Besides having stepped on someone's toes, Papa also mentions that his association with the Chinese in Taiwan didn't help his cause or, as he wrote, "didn't help me either to the ring knockers in career branch."

But if any of that made him bitter, he never showed it, as he set off to do the job he'd been assigned to the best of his abilities.

The story of the 174th, as I've mentioned before, is somewhat overwhelming. I have names and notes and e-mails from people I never would have spoken with prior to Papa's death, and I suppose I can take some small solace that his passing has led me to them. I know that, Papa being the modest man that he was, I never would have heard a lot of the stories that have been sent to me from the men who served with him in Vietnam.

The formation of the 174th is a story I've gotten from a number of people, but it's always the same. As Papa said, it was a "company made up of all equals, or nearly so." Basically, all of the officers were of the same rank. They determined hierarchy based upon date of rank, which is how Papa ended up being in command.

"So I took, right or wrong, the 'collegial' approach," wrote Papa. "We really didn't have a heck of a lot of choice. Without it we would have had open warfare between 'equals.'"

Mr. Cobb sent me this in an e-mail:

> *"As for myself, I reported to Ft. Benning in late October or early November of 1965, with orders to join the 174th AHC. When I arrived, Bob, a senior major, was already there and was the CO. I was next in date of rank, so I was temporarily the Exec. Officer. But, I don't know if that even got on the record because the next day, and for two or three days after that, other majors reported in and some outranked me. When it appeared that everyone on orders for the 174th had reported in, Bob called the most senior majors into the orderly room and said that he was*

ready to make assignments. Because of date of rank among the officers in that unprecedented situation of 32 (give or take a couple) majors in a single company, he would be the permanent CO…"

I can imagine how difficult that would have been for Papa, to have to take command of a group that were more or less his equals. But given the make-up of the soldiers I've talked to from that group, it's clear that none of them would have let something that small get in the way of their mission. There were all highly trained, extremely experienced, and completely committed to what they were doing.

Papa didn't go into much detail on the training process in his letters. He simply wrote that everyone "got the job done, trained, packed, and shipped without too much blood shed…"

Mr. Cobb, however, had a rather tragic anecdote with regards to how they selected positions for everyone. Basically, each ranking member was given the option of choosing the remaining command positions, as CO (Papa), XO, and Service Platoon Commander were all assigned.

The first person up was Major Bill Callanan who was offered the Gunship Platoon. Major Callanan had seven or eight kids and a wife waiting for him, so he declined the position. As near as I can tell, there was no shame in this; he had a large number of mouths to feed, a large number of people dependent upon him for their survival. He'd still be serving his country and supporting his fellow soldiers, just in a capacity that would allow for a greater chance of survival. It wasn't cowardice, it was responsibility to his family.

Instead, Major Callanan was placed in charge of one of the "slick" platoons which carried troops and supplies.

Mr. Cobb was next in line and immediately took the Gunship Platoon.

Here's where the tragic part comes in, and I'll leave it to Mr. Cobb to tell that particular tale:

A sad note here: In November of '66, Callanan, who didn't want the Gunship Platoon Command in the very beginning, was on a major combat air assault mission just west of Pleiku along with the rest of us who were healthy enough to fly. It was a critical mission and everyone was called upon to fly assigned missions. Many of us lost our aircraft due to enemy fire or maintenance problems. The only one in my flight who had made it successfully through the whole day was Callanan and his co-pilot, a young captain named Eugene Smith, who was going home in two weeks to be reunited with his wife and a new baby who Gene had never seen yet. On the last flight of that horrible day, they crashed and died.

Mr. Cobb notes that this had nothing to do with my grandfather, that they were no longer serving together as this point in the war. It does seem like something out of a movie, though, or a Greek tragedy if Greek tragedies were still being written in the 1960s.

This was just one out of thousands and thousands of stories carried around by thousands and thousands of servicemen. Considering that this was Papa's third war, it is amazing to think that he lived as long as he did. As unlucky as I might feel for losing him, Papa led a charmed life.

While Papa was settling in and setting up at Ft. Benning, my grandma and my uncle were moving into an apartment in Kent, Ohio. They moved into a community known as Silver Oaks apartments, significant because years later it would turn into a senior community where my dad's mom would live. Both my dad's parents called it home when they died—albeit briefly for my other grandfather—although their deaths were years apart. Again, there seems to be a certain strange symmetry to these things.

Silver Oaks had a pool, which was what was most important to my uncle at the time.

And just to place the icing on the cake of this conflux of events that was 1965, my mom actually met my dad that fall.

Papa drove up from Fort Benning as often as he could, which was usually once a month. As grandma says, "Once again we were living apart, with only letters to keep us in touch." Papa would get some extended time for Christmas of 1964, but come March of 1965 he was off to Vietnam.

I received a manila envelope from my mom in the mail yesterday. As my parents and Grandma continue to go through my grandparents' belongs, they keep finding more and more things they think might be useful to me as I write this book.

This time around it's a mixed bag of things, including a makeshift booklet with "Major Stuart" hand written across the top. It's entitled "UH-1C, & D Normal and Emergency Procedures, 7th Squadron, 1st Cavalry, July 1967." It's ultimately just a bunch of pieces of paper stapled together at the top. This would have been after his tour in Vietnam.

Next is a full color, twenty-four-page photo book called *The Face of Viet-Nam, the Land and the People*. It's copyrighted 1966 and marked at thirty-five cents. It's clearly a book for a younger audience, perhaps middle school or high school students. It's filled with pictures of the country and a brief description of the culture of its people. There's a two-page spread in the middle of various factions of the U.S. military patrolling the country. On the following page there are servicemen interacting with local people. On the final page there's a photo of the American flag flying side by side with the South Viet-Nam flag and a picture of some South Vietnamese soldiers.

While it could be claimed that this book is meant as propaganda, there's a certain earnestness to it that's hard to criticize. The point of the book is to portray Vietnam as a place that is worth saving, which makes the book a wonderful proponent for a country that many Americans knew nothing about.

Next is a photocopy of Papa's membership application for the Vietnam Helicopter Pilots Association. The photocopy is complete with the date sent in and the number of the check written to pay the $30 annual fee. My grandfather was very organized.

While there's lots of good information on the application, from the types of helicopters Papa flew to the dates of his tour of duty, the most interesting has to be his answer to the "Combat Flight Hours" question: "approx. 300." That's just Vietnam.

Finally, my mom sent along three more pictures. The first is an airborne shot of a U.S. Army L-23D twin engine airplane. There's no date on it and although you can see someone flying the plane, there's no indication of how it's connected to my grandfather.

The next two are obviously connected as they're both photos of Papa, sitting in a helicopter at Ft. Devens. Both are dated 1964, but I have no idea when in 1964, as Papa was stationed at Ft. Devens for that entire year.

It's strange to see these last two photos, particularly the one where he's looking at the camera. He looks exactly as I always remember him, yet this was eleven years before I'd be born, let alone before I'd have any real memory of what he looked like.

That's not what he looked like when he was buried. My grandmother even said as much at the funeral. But I suppose perhaps that's a good thing. I suppose if he'd looked the same as he did when he was alive it would be wrong in some way. He was so vibrant when he was alive that there really wasn't any way he could have looked the same after he passed on.

I've currently made contact with seven different people who served with Papa in Vietnam. The veterans of the 174th have been fantastic. But I'm asking them for details of events that happened four decades ago, events that were often so traumatic even the clearest of minds may have a hard time remembering them. This means that I have to sift through different accounts of the same moments, and I have to do so without Papa's aid.

Bill Haupt was an enlisted man who served under Papa. I believe he's actually working on a book of his own chronicling his time in Vietnam.

Being an enlisted man, Mr. Haupt arrived in Vietnam by ship, arriving at Qui Nhon on the Tonkin Gulf. From there he went to Lane Army Heliport, which would be his new home.

Papa was there to greet him, having flown in earlier. Papa arrived at the end of March, 1966. The arriving troops landed at the beginning of April.

According to Mr. Haupt, the first thing they built at their new base of operations were showers, per my grandfather's instructions. The next thing they built was the Enlisted Quarters, and then the Enlisted Club. Wrote Mr. Haupt: "I guess since Major Stuart had served as an enlisted Marine during WWII he knew how it felt to be on the bottom."

That sounds like Papa. He'd take care of everyone else before taking care of himself.

Mr. Cobb added, "After we arrived in Qui Nhon—Lane Army Heliport—Marty Heuer and a crew of volunteers started building 'hooches' so we could move out of our tents and into more solid structures." Papa's command hooch was large enough to hold four people, so Mr. Cobb, Operations Officer Jim Shrader, and Intelligence Officer Walt Payne bunked in there as well.

Mr. Cobb gave perhaps the best explanation of what life was like, at least on an operational level, in an e-mail he sent me:

Bob, Jim, and Walt worked together every day, Bob running the company and Jim and Walt helping to plan our combat missions and supply missions to the Korean Division and ARVN units which we supported. My mission was, of course, to command the Gunship Platoon and see that our assigned missions were carried out. That kept me either in my hooch resting or on the flight line or in the air. So, Jim and Walt were the closest to Bob on a day-to-day basis at work. At night, when we were all usually relaxing in the hooch after supper, it was just a brief social hour or two and then to bed.

I'm having visions of *M.A.S.H.* again.

According to Mr. Cobb, one of the soldiers assigned to his gunship platoon also played the guitar. So some nights he'd head up to the officers "hooch" and sing and play for Papa and everyone else. I can't help but wonder what kind of songs he played for them. I don't even really know what kind of music my grandfather liked, aside from some Big Band.

My mom sent me an e-mail the other day. I've been forwarding her the messages I've receive from the members of the 174th. She told me that my grandma is putting together a package of papers to send to me. She said that I've become the repository for my grandfather's things. I've evidently become the unofficial keeper of the records of his life.

That's a weird idea to grasp, that I'd be the person solely responsible for the concrete facts of Papa's history. I feel like there's so much that I still don't know, and perhaps never will. But I know the important things.

This is the way my family works. We're fairly guarded people. And while it might serve to keep us away from the world at large, it also serves to make us self-sufficient and resilient.

Papa was just as much a person in my life as he was a figure, a presence. I know that's what he was to the men he commanded in Vietnam as well.

While Papa's composure and presence was felt on their missions, there was perhaps no better example of the quality of his leadership than how he handled a man who went off the deep end.

Mr. Haupt provided a few examples of this, the first being an enlisted man who came into the enlisted "hooch" firing his rifle into the air. Mr. Haupt snuck out of the "hooch" and got my grandfather, who was actually able to get the man to stop firing his gun. He calmed the man down, eventually learning that he'd received a letter from his wife that said she was pregnant. There were only two possible explanations for this: either the soldier had fathered the child before he left, which meant he might never get to see his own son or daughter, or his wife had found someone new while he was stuck in the jungles of Vietnam. Either way, the "I'm Pregnant" letter was like the "Dear John" letter for the WWII servicemen, although this one did twice the damage.

In fact, Mr. Haupt remembers a sergeant who had just been given a promotion who went on a four day bender upon getting an "I'm Pregnant" letter. Needless to say, his promotion didn't hold.

In another case, one of the senior cooks entered the headquarters "hooch" with a live hand grenade in each hand. Once again Papa stepped in and talked the man down. They got the grenades from the man and tossed them away from camp, where both exploded. The cook was drunk, although no one knew exactly where he'd gotten the hand grenades.

"I was beginning to worry," wrote Mr. Haupt, "that I may be KIA by one of our own people."

But that was the way it was, with such a large group of men putting their lives on the line on a daily basis. As Mr. Cobb mentioned, aside from maintaining a strategic position in Vietnam that allowed the U.S. military to launch attack missions at the enemy, they were also supporting both the Korean Division and the Army of the Republic of Vietnam. This would be the same ARVN that flew above the U.S. helicopters instead of below, the one piece of information my grandfather ever gave to my dad about his time in-country.

"We were like a family over there," wrote Mr. Haupt. "He told me once in his hooch that he had a daughter my age and her picture hung over his desk."

Mike Bovre, who not only served under Papa but was Mr. Haupt's bunkmate, added: "Bob was a caring individual who thought first of his men and what he could do for them."

Mr. Bovre also sent me a photo from the 1998 reunion of the 174th AHC featuring himself, Bernie Cobb, and Papa. I actually have a t-shirt from the 2002 reunion that my grandma sent me. They're held every year in Florida.

Papa was particularly straightforward with his men, something which probably added to his reputation as a hard charger; I don't think Papa was always a company man. Mr. Haupt's contract was about to expire and Papa asked him if he was going to re-enlist. At the time, the tax free income was appealing to Mr. Haupt. But Papa told him that if he re-enlisted he'd return to Vietnam at least three more times. "That convinced me to return home," wrote Mr. Haupt. "Time proved him correct. The ones that went over first and re-enlisted would return time and time again."

Papa was with the 174th until September of 1966 when he went to Vung Tau Army Airfield.

"On my next 'fully qualified but no brass ring,'" wrote Papa, "Black Sam pulled my string and down to Vung Tau I went."

"Black Sam" was Lt. Col. Sam Kalagian, the CO of the 14th Battalion.

There's considerably less information available on Papa's time in Vung Tau because the men of that Airfield weren't as closely connected as the men of the 174th. Papa even says as much in a letter to Marty Heuer, another serviceman who was planning on writing a book on his experiences in Vietnam: "Vung Tau supplied all of the I Corps directly or indirectly, had an Aussie CV2 Squadron on the field, assorted TC units, an Air America pad, (a clandestine training camp on the field) plus other odd ball units."

I got the impression that the Vung Tau Army Airfield was a little bit of everything, serving a variety of needs for a variety of people. Because of this, however, it had to be located in the middle of enemy territory. Papa found himself in the thick of it, although they were well prepared for anything that might be thrown at them.

"We had VC all around us," wrote Papa, "but with the Aussies plus a company of Nunas (professional river-bandit soldiers) to call on I never suffered a mortar attack. I would take a bunch of those Nunas commanded by a sp. forces SGT and my HUI to snoop out every likely launch site. Did that about once a week. Fun!"

The best defense, it seemed, was a good offense. I could definitely see Papa subscribing to this philosophy. He had a job to do and the last thing he was going to do was let anyone interfere. Papa was never one to rest on his laurels and he wasn't going to simply sit there and be a target. He was going to be proactive and let the Viet Cong know that any attempts at setting up a spot for mortar attacks would be a bad idea.

Towards the end of 1966, Papa was awarded two more citations, this time, as the article in the Warren Chronicle Tribune states, he "received his sixth and seventh awards of the Air Medal." I really didn't need proof that Papa was successful in the military, but there was a lot of it nonetheless.

Papa was stationed at Vung Tau for six months until he headed back to the States in March of 1967.

Talking to the men of the 174th has been an interesting experience for me. I'm not the most social of people to begin with, so I found that even crafting an e-mail to these men was sometimes difficult. The problem wasn't that I didn't know what to say, it was that I wasn't sure how to say it. Not only did I want to do my family and my grandfather proud, but these were men who deserved my respect. I wanted to make sure they knew that.

Between the various e-mails they sent me and the numerous articles on their website, it's clear that the men of the 174th had, and perhaps still have, no idea what they've done. There's no sense of historical significance with them. There's simply a sense of a job that had to be done and a responsibility to do that job well. At no point do any of them put on airs; none of them are self-aggrandizing.

I started this book pointing out the differences between my grandfather and me. I made note of the fact that I'm a liberal. While many things have changed since I started this project, that isn't one of them: I'm still as liberal as I was when I first sat down at my computer to write the story of Papa's life. And while anyone can argue the merits and lack thereof for the war in Vietnam, nothing—*nothing*—can take away the significance of what these men did.

For me, it's not so much what they accomplished as much as the symbolism of what they did. They believed in something. They were willing to give their lives for something. They were even willing to kill for it. And maybe it was the wrong thing. Maybe their actions were all for nothing and their belief was misplaced. But they shared something beyond what most of us will ever be able to comprehend and they did so with little fanfare. If nothing else, they got us to the point we're at now. They will forever have a place in history, even if they don't realize it.

I don't think that Papa ever did.

14

Civilian Life, Take Two

I CAN SMELL MY GRANDPARENTS' HOUSE. I can smell the basement, at least, which is where Papa kept all of his papers, his photos, and more than likely his medals, although I never saw them until after he died. I can smell it as if I were sitting there right now.

The next time I return home, my grandmother will be living in Kent. She will have sold the house she shared with Papa for nearly thirty-five years. She will have sold most of their furniture in an effort to down size to an apartment. My eighty-year-old grandmother was starting the next phase of her life, just as she had started the last one in that house in Huber Heights.

Moving to Huber Heights, and eventually into that house, would mark my grandfather's second attempt at life outside for the military, and the first attempt that would actually succeed. Like their marriage, the second time was the charm.

On March 18, 1967, Papa returned to Fort Knox from Vietnam. As he said in a letter, "Back to Fort Knox and much as I loved flying and the

141

Army I requested retirement." This was despite the fact that he was, yet again, up for promotion to lieutenant colonel.

"I was in temporary command of the 1st Air Cavalry Squadron, an alerted unit." Evidently, the designated commanding officer was "still in armor" at the Pentagon, so Papa had to do the job. My grandfather always had his own terminology, even beyond military-speak, but I'm guessing that "still in armor" meant that the designated officer was still going through the details of the political side of the job; Papa only ever seemed to mention the pentagon when it involved red tape. But there was Papa, in line yet again for a promotion he'd been passed up for a number of times, actually doing the job for a lieutenant colonel. It seemed as if the Army was like any other business: they'd have you do the work of the higher level job, but they wouldn't give you the raise.

"So again it was requisition, fill, train, etc.," wrote Papa, "till Charlie (the CO) was 'sprung' from DC. Those guys commanding three of those squadrons we trained at Knox, all West Pointers, all shooting for the stars. None made it."

Papa later retracts part of that statement, saying that one of the three West Point trained commanders retired a major general. But I think it's clear that at this point Papa was beginning to wonder what it took to get past the next hurdle in military rank, even if he was trying to put that out of his mind and focus on retirement.

He'd get his answer over the course of his last few months in the Army.

Papa was settling in at Fort Knox. My grandma and uncle actually moved down there from Kent in June of '67. Papa was coasting along to retirement. But, as Papa puts it, "Career branch has suddenly discovered that Vietnam is not going to go away soon."

Over the next few months, Papa began getting telegraphs asking if he was sure that he wanted to retire. They even promised him that he could stay as long as he wanted; there would be no set length of time that he had to stick around for. The kicker, though, came in the form of a phone call just two weeks before Papa's retirement date. "Unofficially (they) tell me," wrote Papa, "that I was first on the next list for LTC in December."

On one hand, it was probably flattering that in such dire circumstances they considered Papa a valuable enough resource to make such promises to him. At the same time, it was clear that they needed officers for the continuing conflict in Vietnam and it was that need that had them making such offers. That need was evidently trumping the reasons they'd passed up Papa so many times over the years. The fact that he'd rubbed people the wrong way over his tenure and spent time with the Chinese no longer bothered his superiors; they needed officers.

"Had it just been me," wrote Papa, "I probably would have caved, but my son was now ten. He needed stability, and our daughter was in college. So goodbye Knox, hello Dayton."

That, of course, was Dayton, Ohio, or more specifically the suburb of Dayton known as Huber Heights.

As Papa said: "Best move I ever made. For once in my life, I made a right decision."

Papa's discharge paper contains a list of the "decorations, medals, badges, commendations, citations, and campaign ribbons awarded or authorized" during the twenty-seven years he was in the Army:

Vietnam Campaign Medal
Vietnam Service Medal
Korean Service Medal
Senior Army Aviator Badge
Letters of Commendation (3)
Letter of Appreciation
Armed Forces Reserve Medal
Army Commendation Medal
Air Medals (7)
National Defense Service Medal
United Nations Service Medal

He enlisted in September of 1942. He retired for good on November 30, 1967 at the age of forty-three. He still had nearly forty years of life left to live.

Whether it was age, experience, or maturity, my grandparents' second attempt as a married civilian couple was much more successful than their first. It was also planned out much better.

Grandma and Papa decided on the Dayton, Ohio area for a number of reasons, not the least of which was the Wright-Patterson Air Force Base, or as my grandmother always called it, "Wright-Pat."

I've been to the Wright-Patterson Air Force Museum a lot, perhaps more than anyone else who isn't either in the Air Force or lives any where near the base. It was something of a staple on our family trips to visit my grandparents. If I had to guess, I would say I was an annual visitor, at least up until I became a teenager. At that point, I think both my grandparents and my parents thought the significance of Wright-Pat would be lost on a misanthropic, hormonal teenager.

I can remember it like it was yesterday, and, to be honest, this is probably the first time I've really thought about those trips in years. I remember that they kept the newer planes outside. I remember that they had old de-signs by the Wright brothers. The younger Wright, Orville, had been born in Dayton, after all. In fact, some Ohio license plates include the slogan "Birthplace of Aviation." I also remember that those informational plaques had nothing on my grandfather; he knew it all.

Wright-Patterson was a fully functioning military base, so it offered my grandparents everything they could ask for as retired military. It's where they would go for surplus goods (I've had my fair share of Military Special whiskey, let me tell you). It was where they'd get their check-ups. It was a way for them to stay connected to that part of their lives and I think in many ways it was a perfect buffer for Papa. He had been career military; he was only forty-three and he wasn't ready to give up that part of his life entirely just yet.

Papa even found a way to keep flying; he joined the Wright-Patterson Air Club.

Huber Heights allowed them to be close to Papa's mom, Goldie, and Grandma's dad, Griffith, in Warren, Ohio, but far enough away to be independent. And they were about four hours away from my mom at Kent State.

For a couple who had spent their lives traveling the world, Hubert Heights would offer them a stability and comfort they had never known. It would be their slice of paradise.

It's the last place Papa would call home.

Papa's second departure from the military mimicked his first in one way: he returned to school.

A few months after my mom graduated from Kent State in June of 1968, Papa began taking classes at Wright State University in Dayton for his MBA. He also worked as the Director of Marketing for a local company called "Beef and Beer," which would have been right up Papa's ally.

I asked my grandmother about B&B and this is the e-mail I received in response:

> *Had not thought about B&B in a long time. Papa got paid in stock which turned out worthless. The wheeler dealer's name was Scanlon, who had visions of a chain of B&Bs... He was on a business trip in a small aircraft, it crashed and he was killed. I don't remember what happened to the pilot and Scanlon's girlfriend. Just as well he was killed as his wife probably would not have been very kind to him.*

B&B probably seemed like a good thing to Papa, who hadn't had a steady job in the civilian world since he re-upped with the military, and whose main work experience consisted of a car dealership, a steel factory, and a soda shop. In the end, however, I think it soured him to the way the business world worked.

Papa then began teaching management classes part time at Sinclair

Community College in Dayton while still pursuing his MBA at Wright State.

My mom, in the meantime, had moved to San Francisco for three months. That didn't seem to work out for her (and I can only imagine what San Francisco in the summer of 1968 was like, given what it was like a year earlier), so she moved back to Ohio, first staying with Goldie. She then moved back to Kent. She was re-introduced to my dad and on May 17, 1969 they were married.

My dad and my grandparents have never been close. The main reason for this, from what I've been able to piece together, is that my parents eloped. As my grandmother so succinctly describes my parents' marriage in her memoirs, "We were notified after the event."

The fact that my brother was born just shy of eight months after my parents were married could not have helped matters.

I'm not sure that my grandparents had met my dad before their daughter married him. This, of course, has led to more than a few awkward moments, not the least of which was my brother's wedding.

A big chunk of our family was there, as well as a few select friends of the family, including my dad's childhood best friend, the man who also served as his best man. He met my grandmother at my brother's wedding and the conversation went like this:

"I was the best man at your daughter's wedding," he said.

"I wish I could have been there," said my grandma.

I, of course, was standing right next to them during this exchange.

I've never asked, but I think my brother and I both figured all of these things out on our own at different times. We'd both be in our twenties before we ever mentioned it to each other.

Given the circumstances, the late '60s were proving to be a tense time for my grandparents.

My uncle, in the meantime, had joined the Civil Air Patrol, a civilian auxiliary to the air force which taught young men how to fly. It seemed like the flying bug had been passed on from one generation to the next. Unfortunately, even though Uncle Rob received his pilot's license at the age of sixteen, he was color blind, which stopped him from being a pilot either in the military or in the private sector. This would be the first of what would be a series of difficulties in my uncle's life.

In January of 1970, my brother Chris was born and Papa became a grandfather. I'm not entirely sure why "Papa" was chosen as a name, since my dad's dad was "Grandpa." The designation fit, though, as he was definitely a "Papa."

Later that year Papa received his MBA from Wright State. The following year he'd receive a full time teaching position at Sinclair and later that year became the chair of the management program, a department that included management, economics, logistics, and, as my grandfather wrote, "a few lesser programs."

In September of 1971 my grandparents moved out of their first home in Huber Heights and into the house they would spend the next thirty-five years in. This would be the only home of theirs I would ever know. It's where they would have their 60th anniversary and where my grandmother currently lives alone. She's recently contacted a real estate agent as she begins the process of moving closer to my parents.

It's almost impossible for me to imagine selling a home of thirty-five years. I can't imagine what my grandmother is going through, although I suppose there's some comfort in knowing that the ghosts that must surround her on a nightly basis will soon be in the past. I honestly can't picture that house without Papa in it. It was surreal when I was there for his funeral and I can't imagine having to walk through it on a regular basis and be reminded of what we've lost.

It's strange to think about that house now. I can remember the lighting in the kitchen, the way my grandmother would leave one light on whenever we spent the night so that I could find my way around if got up to use the bathroom or needed a night time snack. I remember how fantastic I thought the laundry shoot was and that they added a fake fireplace to their bedroom when they expanded the house just a bit.

There was a dining area and there was a living room off the front entrance which my grandparents had decorated in an Asian theme, probably because of all the time they spent in Taiwan. It was filled with amazing, one of a kind pieces that I would imagine would bring in a hefty sack of cash if ever appraised, but I can't imagine my grandmother ever selling them.

We spent almost every Thanksgiving at my grandparents. I'd sit at the bar connected to the kitchen and watch as Papa made his famous potato soup for lunch the day before Thanksgiving. I'd sit there and watch him make his famous stuffing on the actual day. I'd watch as he used some strange, low sugar sweetener in his coffee.

My brother and I would stay in the blue room which is exactly how it sounds: blue carpeting, blue curtains, blue walls, and blue bedding on the two single beds. My parents would stay in the room next door, the room with the organ and a pull out bed. I can remember times when my dad would have to work and my brother was too old to be interested and my mom and I would drive down for a visit and we'd share the blue room, both because the beds were nicer and because she probably wanted to keep an eye on me.

My grandparents always did their best to keep me busy. Papa would take me down to their basement to show me the mishmash of projects they had. They still had the dark room they'd put in for my uncle when he was in college, even though by this point it had been years since he'd used it. Papa would build birdhouses down there for the backyard. There was a desk with a typewriter which I can only assume would mark Grandma's first attempt at writing her memoirs. And, there was the ping pong table.

I can remember playing ping pong with my dad and my brother, but I'm pretty sure that Papa was the first person to ever show me how to play. That table became such a fixture in my life. It became the epitome of my visits. Just writing about it makes me feel like I'm there, in that basement, with its rattan furniture and the old TV, the back laundry room where the dark room was, the office area complete with tiny radio that had no other features—no tape deck, just an AM/FM radio.

The anniversary party last summer was the last time I was there before Papa died.

Because Papa was getting older, they were planning on selling that house. They were going to sell the house and move closer to my parents. Now, with my Papa gone, there's even less reason for Grandma to hold onto it. Selling is the right thing to do, the smart thing to do, but for as much as that house is a part of my life, it's obviously much more a part of theirs. I can't imagine it will be easy for her.

In the next few months Huber Heights—Dayton—will be a thing of the past. It will no longer hold any real significance in the present. It will solely exist, for me, in memory.

15

Storyteller

I WAS BORN WITH A HOLE in my chest.

I entered this world on October 3, 1975, with a *pectus excavatum*, or funnel chest. I wasn't just the second child, but the second grandchild to both sets of grandparents, and such a distinct and, at least cosmetically, severe birth defect must have come as shock, given how healthy my brother was when he was born.

My grandmother had particular reason to be concerned, as the years leading up to my birth had not been kind to her. In 1972, her step-mother, Eleanor, died. Just two years later, Grandma's father, Griffith Davis, would follow his second wife. "He had some heart problems for several years," wrote Grandma, "and after Eleanor died, he lived in a very nice nursing home in Youngstown, Ohio for two years."

Grandma was an orphan at the age of forty-six.

My mom told me that Griffith got to see my brother at least once before he died, which makes me happy. I think it's nice that he got to see his great grandson, even if he wasn't around to see me and my cousin.

My *pectus excavatum* would require surgery, not just to fix my appearance, but also to allow my lungs and heart to grow to their full potential. It was a long process, from pre-op to physical therapy, but it all went well. I still have the scars, not to mention a constant source for family stories.

Maybe that's why I do what I do. Maybe being born with an instant story is what prompted me to start telling them.

I was fortunate to have both pairs of grandparents alive when I was born. I had two grandfathers, yet from early on I liked Papa the best. My childhood is filled with memories of spending time with Papa, with him and my grandma, whereas I can count on one hand the number of details I can remember of my dad's parents' house in Michigan.

I think, as a child, I equated time and attention to affection. My mom's parents knew me better because they were there more often, because they were watching me grow up. It's unfortunate because it created a certain distance between me and my dad's side of the family that wasn't deserved on either end. By the time I was actually spending time with my dad's mom, it was after my dad's father had died, and the sadness she carried with her created a space around her that was almost greater than the distance from Kent, Ohio to Traverse City, Michigan.

Even though I saw them regularly, Grandma and Papa were still more an abstract entity than real people. They brought me gifts and they laughed when I did something funny and they appreciated me just for being there. I felt like I could never do anything to disappoint them. I felt like they'd always be around.

But I suppose that's how most people first learn about death: by losing a grandparent.

In May of 1978, Papa was made a full professor at Sinclair Community College. He was still the chair of the management program, but all the administrative duties were beginning to weigh Papa down. "Tired of administration, so dropped back to classroom only (ten years as chair is enough for anyone unless you're shooting for dean, provost, etc.)."

At the same time, Papa's only son was following in his father's footsteps. My uncle Rob had joined the Navy and was serving on the USS *Enterprise* in the Indian Ocean. He only lasted for a few years, however, and in 1983 became an active reserve.

Grandma sent me a newspaper story about my uncle's time in the Navy. It's a clipping from *The Journal Herald*, which would later merge with the *Dayton Daily News*. It details the USS *Enterprise*, a nuclear powered aircraft carrier, running aground on a sandbar in the San Francisco Bay. After five hours, tugboats and a high tide were able to free the ship.

Accompanying the article is a picture of the aircraft carrier. All of the servicemen aboard are on one side of the deck, evidently in an effort to help the rescue attempts. It's a grainy black and white picture from far, far away. The crew are tiny white specs. Someone, presumably my grandma, has written "See Rob?" above the crew with an arrow pointing down.

In her memoirs, my grandmother says he "would have done justice for a naval career." This was to be only the first of many different paths my uncle would try. Next, he would give college a shot, attending Ohio University, which just happens to be my alma mater. He would renew his interest in photography, but would drop out just shy of graduating.

My grandmother had also decided to give school a try, taking advantage of the free tuition she got at Sinclair. "I took a class for three quarters a year for two years or eighteen credit hours," she wrote in her memoirs. "Through the years I took various classes including: speech, marketing, Psychology of Aging, Music Appreciation and beginning piano lessons after Stu bought me an organ for Christmas."

While academia had been good to them, eventually my grandparents were ready to call it a day.

"Retired (again) in '85," wrote Papa in a letter to an Army buddy. He wouldn't retire completely, though, as he continued to teach part time for two more years. He would also be named Professor Emeritus during those extra two years, the benefits of which included "parking and an office on campus if I wanted."

"Sinclair is a state school," Papa said, "so this was state teachers' retirement." Papa had now put himself in a position to get retirement benefits from the state and federal government, back when retirement money actually meant something. It's amazing that someone who basically led a selfless life—from serving his country in the military to teaching at a community college—would be able to live comfortably after retirement. It's almost a foreign concept these days.

The other day I called home. This, in and of itself, is not really news, although I suppose it probably happens far more rarely than my mother would like. But I had an added bonus in store for her: I was calling to tell her that I'd be coming home for Christmas. I'd even be bringing Nicole with me to boot.

At a certain point it became clear to me that I had to be home for Christmas this year. This was going to be the first year without Papa, and while I might not have seen him last year, the divide between us is obviously much different than it was. Last year I was at least able to call him.

Nicole and I are still at that stage in our relationship where any time apart seems like forever. I'm sure this is part of the honeymoon period. All I know is that boarding a plan without her, particularly when I'm flying to the other side of the country, makes me anxious and more than a little sad.

Nicole felt the same way. I think she also felt that the separation would be the least of my problems. I think she thought, and rightly so, that the first Christmas without Papa was going to be hard for me and that having her there would make everything a little bit easier.

I had assumed telling my mom the news would be the best part of my phone call. I hadn't counted on my grandmother being there with her when I called.

"They're coming for Christmas?" I heard her say in the background. I could tell how happy this news made her. I could picture the look on her face as she asked the question.

But I know that she knows why we're coming home. She knows we're coming home because Papa is no longer here.

I was supposed to be coming home because of Papa, but not like this.

May of 1986 marked the beginning of a new tradition in my extended family: the Davis family reunion.

The first unofficial reunion took place in Gatlinburg, Tennessee, and consisted of my grandmother, her siblings and their spouses. The first expanded reunion would come two years later, as would the idea to have these reunions every other year; a different family member in a different part of the country would host each one.

The funny thing is that even though I was almost fifteen by the time I actually managed to attend a reunion (my parents hosted one in the summer of 1990), it was unclear to me that this was my grandmother's side of the family and not blood relations of Papa's. It just seemed to me that everyone knew and liked Papa, that in many ways he was a focal point of these gatherings because, to me, he was.

It's interesting how the roles of my grandparents' families reversed over time. Papa's family had played a big part in their early lives, particularly his mother, Goldie. But it was my grandmother's family, which had grown larger and larger with each passing year, that would become such a fixture in their lives.

In many ways it also solidified my own immediate family as a unit. My dad's dad died in 1984 and with his mom now living near us in Kent, it seemed to centralize the group of us. But because of the Davis family being the umbrella for the larger family, we were more often than not known as the Stuarts, even though that's not who my brother, my dad, or I were. But that's how we were connected to everyone else. Our branch of the tree ran through Papa.

It's strange to think about it like that, and even stranger because it takes me back to Papa's funeral, to how we were seated in the church, divided so that direct blood relations were in the front pew and extended family in the second, as if a genetic connection was somehow stronger than an emotional one. But I also remember feeling a certain sense of strength there, an unexplainable and almost guilty sense of connection to Papa because I was his bloodline.

At this point there aren't a whole lot of us left.

That first reunion would not be the only time the family would get together during the summer of 1986. The very next month, on June 14th, my uncle Rob got married. I was not quite eleven and my mom dressed me in a blue and yellow suit which probably put me off suits for the rest of my life.

My grandmother, of course, had all the details on the wedding: "We hosted the rehearsal dinner on Friday, June 13, 1986, and they were married in St. Paul Catholic Church on June 14th. After the ceremony, there was a luncheon reception at a Masonic hall. I was pleased to have family attend: Eleanor and Robert; Pat and Ned; and Sherry and David, Chris, and Kyle. Gram Stuart (Goldie) of course stayed several days for her annual visit. Beside their all being invited to the rehearsal dinner, we had them at our house Saturday evening for buffet dinner and conversation."

Uncle Rob's marriage to Jennifer would be a difficult thing to judge over the years, but did give us another addition to the Stuart family: my cousin Megan. "By the time Megan Angharad Stuart came along on April 4, 1989," wrote my grandmother, "we were enjoying retirement and our own little world. Life was good, she added to our joy."

Megan would be the final grandchild and my only cousin.

That same year, Papa, who had kept flying at the Aero Club at Wright-Patterson Air Force Base, finally had to call it quits. As he said: "I was able to fly till about sixty-five out at the Aero Club at WPAFB till high blood pressure zapped my physical (plus developing cataracts, hearing, etc.)."

My uncle's family lived in the next town over from my grandparents, however, so Papa's free time would be filled by his new granddaughter. While he'd only gotten to see my brother and I a few times a year, he'd get to see Megan nearly every day, if he wanted. And knowing Papa, he did. Megan would become very close to my grandparents because of this, one of many reasons why Papa's death was extremely hard on her.

The letter that Papa copied and sent to me was written in 1999. He refers to the decade after he quit flying like this: "Last ten have just enjoyed. Travel, goofing off (I'm good at that!)."

Papa's leaving a lot out. While his military career had been over for twenty years, his family life (and, by extension, mine) would become ever more tumultuous. As the '80s came to an end there were now four generations of Stuarts wandering various parts of Ohio—from Goldie in Warren, to my grandparents in Huber Heights, to my uncle's family in Troy, Ohio, to my family in Kent. In many ways it could be considered our heyday, as it seemed like every one of us were moving forward unto new and exciting things. We were a new kind of army and Papa was our leader.

But, as my grandma said in her memoirs, the '90s would bring "big changes."

16

Big Changes

I CONSIDER THE '90S MY DECADE. I was fourteen when they started and I was twenty-four when they ended. In that time I started and finished high school, started and finished college, and started and was on the verge of finishing graduate school. I was able to drive, vote, and drink during the decade. Most of the firsts in my life happened during that decade.

I know that this country will more than likely never re-capture the anti-establishment vigor of the late '60s/early '70s, just as I know that any comparison to that time is going to seem like a stretch. But for an entire generation, the '90s were just that. Maybe it's just the rose colored glasses of nostalgia, but I can't remember a time in my life when anything seemed possible, and when no one could stop me from doing what I wanted.

For me, the '90s were optimistic and wonderful. I can see how that might be different for my grandfather, though. At the very least he was a lifelong Republican living under a Democratic president.

As I mentioned before, the summer of 1990 marked the first time I would ever attend a Davis family reunion because, conveniently enough, it was held at my parents' house. Since this was only the second official, full blown reunion, the bugs were still being worked out of the system when my parents decided to host, although I didn't really notice.

I remember thinking at the time that the reunion was something that had been going on forever and that I'd just missed them all these years because they were in other parts of the country. My family wasn't big on vacations to begin with, so it made perfect sense that we just didn't go to the reunions unless the reunions came to us. Funny enough, this would actually end up being the case for me, as I'd only attend two more reunions after this one, both of which were in Ohio. The reunion in Atlanta was to be the first one I'd ever gone out of my way to attend. I suppose there's something to that, the idea that I'm just now willing to go out of my way for my family. It goes along with the fact that it took me this long to start writing this book.

I began high school in the fall of 1990, forty-nine years after my grandma and fifty-one years after Papa. Occasional moments of teenage fancy aside, I wouldn't meet the love of my life during these four years.

While I was beginning a new phase of my life, my great grandma or, as I called her, my Big Grandma, Goldie Stuart, was nearing the end of hers. She had a stroke in March of 1991 and died on May 3rd at the age of ninety-three.

When my dad's father had died years earlier, I wasn't really old enough to understand much of what happened, or at least I wasn't old enough to store it in my head. I have a few memories, like my mom trying to explain to me what death was and where my grandfather had gone. I have a vague memory of sitting in a pew and someone I'm assuming was my brother pointing out to me that my dad had yet to cry. But these are musty and faded memories, as coherent and significant as the dreams I had two weeks ago. I don't remember enough to decipher them.

Big Grandma was different, though. Although I didn't see her on a regular basis, I was old enough to know her. I remember that she had a metal cane with four pronged feet and that she sometimes made a clucking noise with her teeth when she ate. She had a cookie jar on her kitchen counter that was filled with dog treats and every once in a while she'd let me give them to her dog. When I was hungry, she'd always give me Wheat Thins, which was strange for me because my parents never bought them. Now that I'm an adult, I buy them all the time, a regular reminder of my great grandmother.

My parents bought me my first comic book when we were visiting Big Grandma. Decades later, I have boxes of them everywhere.

My mom told me that Big Grandma died and that we'd be driving to Warren. I lay in bed that night trying to understand what that meant, that she'd died. I knew what it meant in a general sense, but I didn't know what it meant to me specifically, or how it would affect my family.

The service marked the second time in five years that I wore a tie. Although I might not remember exactly what I wore, I know it wasn't the yellow and powder blue number my mom had put together for me years before, something I was now old enough to be thankful for.

I remember sitting in a black folding chair during some sort of service. And I remember being in Big Grandma's house which felt strange to me because she was no longer there.

I don't remember ever seeing my mom cry. Knowing what I know now, I suppose that was strange. I have to believe that my mom did cry and either she was hiding it from me or I managed to be oblivious enough not to notice.

I don't remember Papa at all, not during those days. I honestly couldn't say if he was upset or not because he's not in my memory at all. I think that was the point, actually. I think that he was so busy with getting Big Grandma's estate in order, with taking care of the funeral and everything that would come after, that he managed to remove himself from the reality of the situation. I'm not saying that to imply he was in denial or anything like that because for all I know he was off somewhere with my grandmother just trying to cope with the loss of his mother.

I don't remember my grandmother during this time, either, and I'm guessing it was for much the same reason. Even as Big Grandma had naturally grown apart from my grandparents as they got older, I think history still weighed pretty heavily. Goldie was, after all, the only family member at my grandparents' wedding. My grandmother doesn't even mention Big Grandma's death in any real detail in her memoirs, aside from the date and the cause.

A lot of this is speculation, of course, based on memories that are fifteen years old. But I can rather definitively remember never seeing my grandparents or my mom cry during those few days and I can remember walking around not really sure if I was supposed to be crying or not.

From all accounts, my great grandmother Goldie took on the role of head of the household after Seth died and after Papa returned back to duty. Goldie seemed to be one of those defining women of her generation, the ones who paved the way for so many strong women after her. It really is no wonder to see how that line has progressed, from my grandmother to my mom to my brother's wife. She set the trend of raising strong women and men who sought out strong women to add to the family.

I know not many people get to know a great grandparent, let alone have one in their life for fifteen years. I know how lucky I am.

Unfortunately, Papa would soon be the last remaining member of his nuclear family. My grandmother wrote: "It almost seemed like Stu's sister Betty Kagy Bock had suffered through many years of poor health, but hung on until after her mother had died, before giving in to death herself. By fall, she was back to her beloved Florida Keys where she succumbed Nov. 16, 1991."

As I mentioned a while back, I know very little about my mom's aunt, aside from the fact that she was a nurse and that she exchanged letters with my grandfather when he was in basic training.

I don't remember her at Big Grandma's funeral, although as proven above that doesn't particularly mean anything.

I think I might be reading too much into the lack of information regarding my great aunt. My brother and I aren't significantly close, so perhaps there wasn't much for Papa to say. And I don't know that I'd include a great deal of detail on my in-laws if and when I write my own autobiography. Aside from Goldie, my grandmother doesn't talk about Papa's family to any real extent, so perhaps the lack of detail on Betty is simply because she's a secondary character in this story.

Still, she played a pivotal role in Papa's life; the letters he sent her when he was in basic training have given me a glimpse of what he was going through, and for that I am extremely grateful.

In the span of six months Papa became an orphan and lost his only sibling. That had to take a toll. But if it did I never saw it, as my grandfather was the same as he'd ever been the three to four times a year I would see him.

In the spring of 1992, my grandfather gave me a car. More to the point my grandfather gave me his mother's car, a 1972 brown Ford Pinto with 20,000 miles on it. Big Grandma had only ever used it to drive to the grocery store and to church. Ford quit making Pintos because they had a tendency to explode when rear-ended by anything going over thirty-five miles per hour. They're also really, really ugly cars.

Papa had put a substantial amount of time and money into the car, because even though it had only a few miles on it, time had taken its toll. Specifically, rust had taken its toll, to the point where Papa had to have an entire door replaced. I can't imagine it's easy to find a replacement door for a '72 Pinto, but by the time it showed up in my driveway it was about as pristine as such a car could be.

I thanked my grandfather for the car immediately and took it for a drive.

Later that day my mom asked me if I'd thanked Papa for the car.

"Of course, as soon as he gave it to me," I said.

"You should thank him again," she said. "He doesn't always hear very well."

I did and I felt bad that he'd gone most of the day thinking I hadn't said anything. At the time, I assumed Papa's hearing problem was due to his age. I had no idea it was caused by a lifetime around large engines. He'd probably begun losing the extreme ranges of his hearing when he was in the South Pacific. He'd probably spent most of his life with some level of damage to his ears.

Most of my high school life was dependent on that car, on my great grandmother's car that my grandfather had passed down to me. I treated that car horribly.

Maybe I can redeem myself by including it in this book.

I saw my grandparents on a fairly regular basis in the first part of the '90s, for most major holidays and then a few times otherwise. I think high school was such a giant force in my life at that point that everything else seemed secondary. I don't think I ever really gave my grandparents a second thought. I would see them four times a year and I would enjoy seeing them but that was more or less the extent of it.

I can remember times after I got my drivers' license that we'd drive to my grandparents for a few days. I can remember that, without fail, I'd ask to borrow the car keys so that I could drive to the local comic book store. At the time I thought that every store was different and it was something of a quest of mine to discover as many as I could. Not only that, but I was always able to find a new batch of really cheap comics that I could buy to keep myself entertained during our stay.

In the spring of 1994 I graduated from high school. I got money and school supplies as graduation presents.

I headed off to college, initially attending a small, private school in the middle of Ohio. It was also a conservative school, which I would imagine probably made my grandparents pretty happy, particularly in the middle of a fairly liberal decade. I'd only last a year there, though, before transferring to a large public school with a reputation for partying, Ohio University.

The fall that I headed to college my brother started a teaching job at the local middle school, the same one he and I had both attended. My brother had gone to Kent State just like my parents and was officially now a productive member of Kent society, something of a "legacy" if such a thing existed for residents of suburban towns.

But while one of Papa's children seemed to be thriving and raising a successful family of her own, the same could not be said for the other.

My uncle Rob had been in and out of jobs for as long as I could remember. His wife, Jennifer, seemed to be able to hold onto her job at a bookstore, but a young daughter demanded more than a single income could supply. At one point Rob became the manager of the Arbor Gate motel which gave him not just a job, but a place to live. Unfortunately, when he lost that job he also lost his family's home.

I remember having breakfast at my grandparents' house one time and my mom and Grandma talking about my uncle. I remember my grandma informing us that Uncle Rob had taken the civil servants test to work at the post office and had failed. My mom mentioned that it was because my uncle probably blew through the test, not taking the time to actually read the questions. General consensus was that my uncle, whether correct in this assumption or not, considered himself too smart for most people, and this would be his undoing.

Ultimately, though, it wasn't his ego so much as it was his drinking.

I sometimes wonder about the relationship between Papa and his only son. I saw very little of it as I was growing up, aside from my uncle's meandering life and his slow descent. At some point, though, the father has to ask himself if he's done something wrong. At some point I'm sure Papa wondered if he'd done something to cause his only son to end up the way he did.

I would imagine there was a certain amount of pressure on my uncle Rob to be a military man, but I don't know that the pressure was overt. But I also know that Rob's formative years were inundated with what can only be described as Papa's legacy.

I think early on it was a positive influence. As I mentioned earlier, Rob took an interest in flying at an early age, only to see any hopes of being in the Air Force ruined by his eyesight. But he definitely had one of Papa's passions, which is an amazing thing for a father and son to share. But that didn't last long.

It's funny: When I called Marty Heuer, who had served under Papa, he asked me if I had ever served in the military. I answered quickly that I had not, but my mouth (as often times is the case) was moving far quicker than my brain. In my head I was dwelling on the question because my answer actually made me feel a bit unworthy. Here I was, the grandson of a three war veteran yet I was a member of the first generation of my family to never serve in uniform. I almost felt like I wasn't good enough to be talking to Mr. Heuer, like I wasn't good enough to be writing this book.

And that was just one phone conversation with a man I never met, a man who wasn't a retired major. A lifetime under the shadow of my grandfather must have had an impact on my uncle..

Part of it, I'm sure, was generational. Papa's life had been pretty well laid by the military. If there were grey areas, like meeting and marrying Grandma, Papa seemed to just instinctively know what he wanted and how to get it. The biggest grey period of Papa's life was when he left the Marines and he remedied that by joining the Army. The military gave Papa's life structure.

Rob had more options. He turned eighteen in 1975 and there was no war waiting for him. When he graduated, he didn't find himself debating whether or not he should enlist. He could do anything he wanted, but I don't think he knew what that was. My grandparents weren't really in a position to understand that and my mom, regardless of the twists and turns her life would take, had gone from high school to college to marriage to mom with few breaks in between. My uncle was in uncharted territory.

But it would be patently false and reprehensible to place the bulk of any blame on Papa's shoulders for what became of my uncle, of his son.

While I'm sure his legacy was a lot to live up to, at some point my uncle had to make his own choices, whether those choices came from under a shadow or not. My grandparents might not have been perfect parents, but it was clear they did more right than wrong. I know this because of how my mom turned out and because of how she treats me in return.

My grandparents tried to help my uncle at every turn and Rob was given every opportunity to turn his life around. But for some reason he never seemed willing or able to do it.

Rob may have been a grown man, but his daughter was just a child. This was Papa's concern. I don't know how things would have played out had Rob not had Megan, but because he did my grandparents were much more likely to intervene.

In January of 1995, my uncle had a lump removed from his neck. To this day I don't know what that lump was, but considering he smoked Marlboro Reds as long as I knew him, I'm sure chances were good it was cancerous.

Just two months later, Rob was hospitalized with pancreatitis and a lung infection. The pancreatitis was caused by his drinking, while the lung infection was most likely brought on by his smoking. If there were ever a double punch wake-up call for his lifestyle, this would have been it.

I can remember my mom stopping to see me at college on her way back to Kent from visiting my grandparents in Dayton. She stopped to fill me in on my uncle. She told me that he'd been released from the hospital and that he would go into some kind of program for his drinking. That last part was an assumption on her part, and not a safe one. From what I can remember, no one ever really pushed the issue.

As my grandma says in her memoirs, "As he came from the hospital he lit a cigarette, the worst thing for his very tenuous condition, but he knew that."

I think it was clear to my grandparents that they couldn't count on Rob to take care of their granddaughter. The following year, with Rob and Jennifer both unable to hold steady jobs and finding themselves on the verge of eviction, my grandparents bought them a house.

I don't know the details of the arrangement, but I can only assume that my grandparents charged my aunt and uncle some minimal amount of rent. I would also assume that an unspoken quotient of the deal was that my grandparents had unquestioned access to their granddaughter.

The idea, in theory, was that without having to worry about rent and with a built in support system for taking care of their daughter, my aunt and uncle would be able to pull their lives together. And while they would periodically make some headway, it never seemed like they were willing to do what it would take to change their ways. Or, at least, my uncle seemed unwilling.

The year wasn't entirely filled with drama, though. "We celebrated fifty years of marriage on June 22nd of that year," wrote Grandma. "We went to the 'Inn at Honey Run' a nature oriented, but very comfortable place for an overnight stay. Stu gave me a beautiful gold cross with diamonds. We certainly felt blessed to have had so many years together, but especially to have been apart and then found our way back together for a very full and interesting life."

In 1998 I graduated from college only to go directly to graduate school. Evidently, academia to me was like the military for Papa. I think that's a fair comparison, actually, as graduate school gave me much the same things: a steady paycheck, some structure, and the chance to meet interesting people. Add in travel and constant chance of death and we'd have a match.

Symmetry again showed up, as my brother entered the next phase of his life as well. He married his wife Wendy that summer. It was an outdoor wedding and it rained like crazy.

Fortunately, the downpour held off until after the ceremony, but the entire reception was being held outside under a big tent. It rained so hard, so quickly, that the ground was unable to soak up all the water. While the storm itself was relatively short, the wedding party and all the guests found themselves surrounded by a few inches of standing water.

This, however, only served to make the reception that much more fun. People simply took off their shoes and socks and sloshed around in the water and mud. It was the ultimate icebreaker. The steady stream of alcohol probably helped, too.

At the end of the night, we even managed to get what I think ended up being the last group photo of our immediate family (complete with an ex-girlfriend of mine that my mom would later have digitally removed). But there we were, the newly weds, my parents, my grandparents, my dad's mom, my uncle, his wife, and their daughter.

After the difficulties we'd had earlier in the decade, this wedding seemed like a great way to see it out. Heading off to graduate school, I thought that perhaps the extended Stuart family would finally get a few breaks, or at least know some relative calmness.

I was wrong.

17

Perspective

THE ONE, DIRECT PIECE OF ADVICE that my grandfather ever gave me involved whiskey.

It was Christmas of 2000. I had moved to Atlanta after I graduated from college for a second time, this time with a post-graduate degree in the ever-impressive field of Creative Writing. There were only tenuous reasons for choosing the jewel of the South, the most important of which being I had a friend there who'd I'd gone to school with and who could play the drums (as I played the guitar). He also let me sleep on his floor until I found an apartment and a job.

While the story of the two years I spent in Atlanta could fill a separate book entirely, as always, it's Christmas that's important. This year my visit home required vacation days from work, so I had a very small window for my trip. I would have to fly in on the 23rd and fly back out on the 26th.

This ninety-sixish-hour whirlwind meant that I had to cram a lot of visiting into a little time. The side effects of this, for the purposes of this story, were twofold: 1) my grandparents made the drive up to Kent and spent the actual holiday of Christmas at my parents' house, thus eliminating the bi-annual rotation of trips; and 2) I had to see all of my friends from high school in one night.

So it was, on Saturday, December 23, 2000 that my friends and I headed to the bars in downtown Kent.

And I proceeded to drink a lot.

Like most stupid college kids, I drank stupid things. Back then it was pretty much always Jack and Coke, although that night it was mixed with a never ending series of shots. This is what old friends—particularly males—do when they see each other after a long absence: shots. Towards the end of the night I switched to beer, as my addled brain believed that moving to something with less alcohol would allow me to avoid spending the night throwing up.

I then proceeded to walk the two miles from the bars to my parents' house... In December.

In Ohio.

Like I said, I'd yet to out grow my college stupidity. The fact that I didn't get pneumonia is probably a minor miracle.

I then spent the night hugging a trash can that I'd brought to bed with me. I did manage to avoid throwing up...

...until the next morning.

At one point, probably around ten or so, I was on the floor next to the bed with the trash can in my arms. I'd already thrown up quite a bit and there was no sign of an ending any time soon. My mom came into the room and, from her vantage point, could only see that I was on my knees next to the bed. She thought I was looking for something.

"Did you lose something?" she said.

The correct answers there were either "my cookies" or "my dignity."

I was in bed until six o'clock that evening.

So it was that Papa came to bestow upon me his tip on drinking: "It's not the alcohol that makes you sick," he said, "it's the sugary stuff you mix it with."

I like to think that Papa was talking about more than just drinking. I like to think that he was talking about how to lead a successful life. He knew that there are things that matter in this world and there are things that don't and the most important lesson you can ever learn is how to distinguish between the two. Because the things that matter don't make you sick. It's the extra, the excess, the superfluous and irrelevant that trips you up and makes life harder.

This was a lesson he learned early, a lesson that was reinforced often, particularly during the sixty years he spent with my grandmother. I think it was their ability to prioritize that helped make their marriage so successful, even if it did take them more than one try to get it right—and more than one try to even start.

From then on out my only mixer was to be gloriously pure water. Not only have I not gotten sick since then, I've rarely even gotten a hangover, much to Nicole's consternation. On top of that, no one else in the family drinks whiskey and water. It's a little thing that Papa and I shared exclusively; something that, in the end, brought me some small amount of comfort.

There's been some debate on how I'm going to handle 2002. I comprise both sides of that debate and while most of it was internal, Nicole has been very good about the parts that I verbalized when she's in the room. She's very accepting about the fact that I sometimes use her as a sounding board.

Papa saw a lot in his lifetime. I've managed to see a little. I'm relatively sure that 2002 was the worst year either of us has ever lived through, and I make that claim with the understanding that Papa served in three wars.

Not all of what happened was about my grandparents directly, which is why I debated how much of this particular story to tell. But in the end it's about family and family is important. In the end, the story of any one of us is still Papa's story, still Grandma's story. It all ties together.

My grandmother describes the start of the year, perhaps better than I could:

Thursday, January 3, 2002, a day that began with an abrupt phone call at 6:30 AM—interrupting sleep on a dark winter morning. However the message I heard as I answered quickly, hoping not to disturb my husband and to set the caller straight that they had a wrong number, finished my awakening with a jolt. "Jennifer died this morning" were the blunt, no nonsense words I heard. Shock not withstanding, Mother type questions came from my lips and just as matter of factly, my son assured me all had been done and the terrible truth was just what he had said. "We'll be right there" was my reply.

My aunt Jennifer had been in the shower as my cousin Megan got ready for school. When I think about it, I imagine my uncle making breakfast. He's always enjoyed cooking and, as he was still unemployed, it seemed like that would have been his role in the morning.

Jennifer had been in the shower for a while, so Megan decided to go tell her to hurry up or they'd be late.

Megan found her mother on the floor in the shower.

My grandparents arrived to find an ambulance on the scene, but the outcome had already been determined. Their main concern was to take Megan back home with them, to get her away from that house and that scene.

"What was going through her mind," my grandmother wondered about Megan in her memoirs, "as the memory of seeing her mother collapsed in the shower, already beyond recall, must have replayed over and over. 'Lord, I need wisdom to say and do what she needs this day. And for many days to come as we begin an unexpected journey' was my prayer."

To this day I have no idea what killed her.

Part of the drawback of being in a laconic family is that information like this, information that's unpleasant and, ultimately, over and done with, tends not to get passed around like perhaps it should. We also don't ask a lot of questions in such cases. My grandparents might have known what happened, but I'd never be able to ask them. That's just not the way it works. I don't know if my grandmother would even want to tell me if asked. I think part of me is afraid of how she would respond if I did.

I wasn't close to my aunt. I saw her once a year and I never had that many conversations with her. I remember playing euchre with her, my uncle, and my brother one time. She was on my team and I went alone on the last hand and ended up with the five highest cards, winning us four points for the win. I also remember that she and my uncle were really into Hootie and the Blowfish and that she used to work in a book store, which I always thought was cool.

But I didn't really know her.

When my mom called me to tell me that she'd died I was shocked and saddened and concerned for my cousin. And I was really concerned for my uncle, because at that point no one really knew if drinking was still a problem for him. I think we were all relatively sure he still drank, but I don't think any of us allowed ourselves to comprehend that any drinking was a problem.

I was still living in Atlanta, flitting from job to job as those in their early twenties are wont to do. I didn't make it back to Ohio for my aunt's funeral.

That was how 2002 started; it would get progressively worse.

I remember that they had to give my brother's wife magnesium and that it made her extremely sensitive to light and that she basically had to lie in a dark room doing nothing but trying not to go into labor. It was only April and if Wendy went into labor the twins would be born too early to survive.

We'd try to make jokes to relax ourselves. We'd say that this would be a great story to tell the boys when they grew up. This was the ultimate "labor" story. Wendy was basically bringing them to term by sheer force of will.

My brother didn't have a cell phone and he was almost always at the hospital. I was still in Atlanta and my mom told me there was nothing I could do, nothing anyone could really do but wait. I sent my brother an e-mail telling him I'd do whatever he wanted. My brother and his wife were in danger of losing their children and all I could do was send him an e-mail.

Wendy held out as long as she could—longer than I think anyone could—and the doctors, fearing for everyone involved, finally performed a C-section on May 6, 2002. My nephews Nathan and Connor were born two months early at only twenty-eight weeks.

The next few weeks were touch and go. Every moment of good news was followed by one of bad and every time we thought they'd be okay something would happen to suggest the opposite.

With all of this going on, the fact that my grandmother, my dad's mom, was going into the hospital again for surgery was never even mentioned to me. Again, I think my parents were trying to protect me. They were giving me filtered information. Unfortunately, there were other things going on in my life that even they didn't know about, things that were making the situation harder to deal with.

On Sunday, May 12th, my then-two-year relationship with my girlfriend ended. It did not end well and there was a lot of crying involved. My mom called me that day and I withheld that information from her, because it was Mother's Day and she had enough things to worry about. I didn't want her to worry about me.

I never said I was exempt from my family's traits.

Five days later I decided to update my journal fully, as up until that point I'd only made one comment about the end of my relationship. This was part of what I wrote:

And it got worse. Last night I talked to my parents. My grandmother (my dad's mom) died this week. And on top of that, my nephews, who were born prematurely, are not doing very well. My mom said that "it doesn't look good."

So, obviously, I'm drunk right now. I've been drunk a lot this week, something I'm sure my liver is not too thrilled about. And there's lots and lots more that I should write about—my upcoming last week of work followed by my last few days in Atlanta, my extended stay in Kent before I fly out west, the terror of having to make it in LA on my own, the feeling that I've betrayed everyone I care about by being away from them—but I'm just tired. I don't have the energy to be philosophical. I don't have the energy to be deep. I just want to drink my whiskey and not think about my life for a few hours.

I was told that doctors did not expect my nephews to make it through the week. I was told that my grandmother had died. And I walked around my apartment, the one that I had, up until recently, shared with my girlfriend, with a bottle of Jack Daniels in one hand and a phone in the other.

I'd lost two family members so far this year and from what I'd been told I was soon to lose two more before they'd even had a chance to live, before I'd ever even met them.

For some time I'd been planning on returning home for a few weeks before moving to Los Angeles. At this point, however, I had no idea what I would find when I got there.

I believe that there are certain aspects of the universe that are beyond human comprehension. I think it's egotistical for us to think that we can conceive of everything around us. I firmly believe that half of life is perception and that perception can determine reality. I may not believe in a specific God per se, but I'm not so self-righteous as to believe that mankind can understand everything the universe has to offer.

To this day I firmly believe that my nephews are alive because my grandmother died.

In July of 2004 my brother and his wife took a vacation. Part of their trip took them to San Diego, so I drove down to spend the day with them.

There was a good group of us, between my brother, Wendy, her brother, his boyfriend, and me. Their flight back to Arizona (where Wendy's brother lived) was a few hours off, so we decided to have dinner at a Mexican restaurant in Old Town San Diego.

At some point during the conversation the issue of my grandmother's death came up. Wendy and I apparently saw eye to eye.

"I firmly believe that her dying had something to do with the boys living," I said.

"So do I," said Wendy with a slight tone of disbelief. I'm perhaps the least religious member of my family, so I think she was surprised that I would say such a thing.

"The timing of it is just too strange."

"I tell Chris the same thing," she said.

My dad's mom knew that the twins had been born. That was more or less the extent of what she was able to learn before she had her surgery, the surgery that would ultimately cause her death, although not by any fault of the doctor. She'd lived a long life and the dangers were well known to everyone.

She died on a Monday. Two days later my mom called to tell me the boys wouldn't make it past Friday. The following Sunday she called to tell me they had shocked everyone and were doing well.

I don't know how to explain such a thing. The more literal part of me pictures my grandmother's spirit floating in the ether and visiting my nephews one night, touching them on their foreheads and giving them whatever bits of life she was able to carry with her to the other side.

The bottom line is that my grandmother died and my nephews survived. And I don't believe in coincidence.

I didn't talk to my grandparents much during this time. Neither of them were particularly close to my dad's mom. They'd loved my aunt as they loved anyone who joined their extended family. The biggest concern for everyone involved was for the children, both my cousin Megan, who was alive and dealing with the sudden death of her mother, and my nephews who were still in the NICU in tiny incubators.

I made it home at the end of May 2002, in time for my grandmother's wake. I spent two weeks at home before moving to Los Angeles and in that time I was able to visit my nephews in the hospital. They were so small. It was clear that they were still supposed to be inside Wendy, that they'd entered this world too soon.

I suppose that's what 2002 would come down to: timing. Everything was happening too soon. People were being born too early. People were dying before their time. And I was constantly elsewhere.

My uncle and his daughter were still living in the house my grandparents had bought for them. I don't know how they were managing, how they were coping. At that point they really only had my grandparents to turn to and even they had to split their attention. My uncle was an adult and should have been able to deal with things himself. My nephews were weeks old and they needed all the help they could get.

I wonder if the timing of everything made it easier for my uncle to slip away or if it would have been inevitable regardless.

On Sunday night, July 28, 2002, my uncle went to bed.
He never woke up.

From my grandmother's memoirs, this is how it happened for my grandparents:

An ordinary Monday, July 29, 2002, with usual chores. Called Rob several times, always got a busy signal… About 1:00 Megan called us and said she couldn't wake up her Daddy. I told her to call 911 and we'd be right there… As we drove over, I think we both knew it was not good, and the 12-15 minute drive was a quiet one. By the time we arrived, it was all decided—the police and medics had done their job, but the soul was gone from the earthly body.

Megan had twice been on the scene of parental death. Now she was 13, a very impressionable age, a very tenuous age, certainly more trauma than a girl of those years should have to endure.

And so we cry, for her and for ourselves, as we go through the motions of accepted procedure. Usually, I don't look at dead people, they look so different, but Rob looked so good, so like his old self and so peaceful. Lord, I pray he is in your care and finally at peace.

I had moved to Los Angeles in June and not two months later my mom called me to tell me the news. As bad as it sounded initially, it would gradually get worse.

On that Monday morning, my cousin went into her dad's room to wake him up. And she found him dead. For the second time in six months she discovered one of her parents dead.

My grandparents had lost their only son.

You see things in movies and on TV and read things in books about how the worst pain a parent can go through is burying a child. Papa had been the only son and he followed in his father's footsteps to a certain extent. My uncle chose a different path, but he was still his father's son. Whether we accept it or not, sons carry with them the burden of their father's hopes and dreams, they carry the weight of a life that could have been. And while that might cause estrangement, it also creates a bond that's singular to boys and their dads.

I've been fortunate enough to have some help with that load, but that doesn't mean it isn't there.

How could my grandparents have felt by this point? From buying my uncle a house to taking care of their granddaughter, my grandparents had done whatever they could to try to help my uncle right himself. It must have torn them up.

But there would be recriminations enough for everyone.

Weeks later my mom sent me an e-mail explaining to me that the official cause of death for my uncle had been organ failure. Evidently, his body had just shut down while he was asleep. It shut down from years of alcohol abuse.

"But with Rob," wrote Grandma, "we hadn't been able to see the serious problem building in his life. It wasn't new, it had been building over a long period—poor health and bad habits that made his health worse...."

To this day I often wonder if I could have done something. I even wrote a short story about it, a piece that actually describes my uncle as an alcoholic, the first time such a label had ever really been placed on him by anyone in my family. My entire family has read that story and since then both of my parents have been more at ease saying as such, but it's still not something that comes up in conversation, it's not something that's mentioned when my uncle's name arises.

I hope that my grandparents didn't wonder if they could have done more and yet I know that they must have, at the very least during the time just after his death. Because I know that I spent hours wondering what I could have said to him, coming up with poignant speeches that would have gotten through to him and made him realize that he had to stop drinking not just for his own sake, but for his daughter's as well. But I never said those words—no one ever said those words—and I'm not sure they would have made a difference, anyway.

My grandparents had two children. One spent his life bouncing from job to job. He drank a lot and smoked a lot and ended up in the hospital more than once. He drank himself to death and left behind a young daughter with no parents. The other might have done a few crazy things in her lifetime, but she managed to have a career and to have a family and to stay in touch with her parents. And she's still with us and has two boys who are all grown-up and doing well. She even has two miracle grandchildren.

It's not for me or anyone else to say why one child went one way and one child went the other. And I hope that my grandfather didn't spend the remainder of his life trying to figure that out.

I realize that it's strange for me to talk about drinking whiskey and how I consider that a connection to my grandfather. I know it's strange to say such things when my uncle, Papa's only son, was an alcoholic. But alcohol was simply a means to an end for my uncle; it wasn't the problem, it was his misguided attempt at a cure. During the holidays my grandfather would make my mom and Grandma "Planter's Punch" and he'd pour whiskey and water for the two of us and we'd relax and talk and drink. But it was never an escape for us. It was never the answer to a problem we didn't understand.

Unfortunately, 2002 wasn't done with us yet.

I'm paraphrasing, but this is how my dad's end of a phone conversation went a few weeks later:

"The minister from our church called to see how I was dealing with my mom's death. I told him I really hadn't had time to deal with it, as I was packing to go to my brother-in-law's funeral and I'd just been diagnosed with prostate cancer."

In my family this is what's known as a "humorous anecdote." We don't actually call them that, but that's how serious news is delivered—in passing, with a joking tone. And, honestly, after the year we'd had, could you really blame us?

I didn't go to my uncle's funeral, just as I'd missed my aunt's funeral. Instead I sat in my apartment and digested the fact that my dad had cancer.

It had actually gotten to the point where hearing the phone ring made me nervous.

I'm sure my parents kept this information to themselves when they went to the funeral. After all, my dad was still with us. They'd caught it early and they'd start treatment soon. My uncle was gone and he was never coming back.

It was only recently that I saw my uncle's grave. I only saw it because Papa now rests next to him.

Since I missed my uncle's funeral, I also missed my grandfather. I have no idea how he was dealing with everything that had happened. I wouldn't see him until that Christmas and by that point months had past and my nephews were home from the hospital. The tragedies of the past year were no longer foremost in our minds. My nephews, these two new additions to the dwindling family line, were what mattered.

My family transformed that year, so much so that we were able to hold it together when my nephew, Connor, was diagnosed with cancer in August of 2003. He was only fifteen months old. He went through chemo and had surgery to remove the tumors. He actually made it home in time for Christmas that year and he's been cancer free since then. He and my dad participate in the cancer survivors walk every year.

In the end, 2002 became the watermark for crisis in my family. It was the year that redefined "perspective." It was a year that would help us get through the trials to come.

PART THREE

Ellipsis

18

Winter

MY GRANDMOTHER MOVED INTO HER NEW apartment this week. My parents drove down to Huber Heights on Monday. My dad loaded up his van with the most valuable items and drove back up to Kent that same day. The next day the movers came and my mom drove my grandmother back. As my mom pointed out, she would be doing the driving because she imagined my grandma would be unable to focus on much as they left.

My grandma eventually decided on an apartment at Silver Oaks, the same community she lived in with my uncle nearly forty years ago. The apartment is not quite a mile from my parents' house and on the way from their house to my brother's. She went with a three bedroom apartment so my cousin would have a room there. My parents' bought her a microwave for Christmas as her old microwave stayed with the house.

I can't imagine starting a new phase of your life at that age, not after everything Grandma's already been through.

According to my mom, Grandma got rid of a lot of stuff before the move, but still had to get rid of even more when she moved into the new place. The weather wasn't too bad, though, so they managed to get everything done with as little difficulty as possible. Last night was Grandma's first night alone in the new place.

Winters in Ohio can be incredibly depressing. They're stark and grey and the heavy malaise that hangs over everything only serves to make life seem harder. The one saving grace is that, according to something my dad read, 70% of the time there's snow on the ground on Christmas Day in Ohio. The one saving grace is that there's this beautiful white cover to the world that hides the grey, that turns the sullen and difficult winter into something picturesque and borderline inspirational.

As of right now, however, the forecast for Christmas calls for rain.

For me, the most tangible part of Papa being gone is the space he left behind.

Christmas was strange, but not in the way I figured it would be. Ohio was unforgiving; it never snowed and it was bleak and rainy most of the time. Nicole got her first real taste of freezing rain, something every Ohioan knows intimately. The sun never came out. Nicole and I would get a full night's sleep, but were never really able to wake up the next day. We finally realized that it was because there was no sign of the sun, no indication that the day had actually begun. We were so accustomed to actual sunshine to signify the start of a new day that without it our minds and bodies slipped into a fugue state.

We spent Christmas Eve at my brother's house. This was something of a symbolic gathering, at least from my perspective. Aside from last Christmas, when I was at Nicole's parents' house, I have spent every Christmas Eve at my parents' house. Even after my brother and Wendy had the boys, my parents' house remained grand central station for my family. This only made sense, as it was not only where I was staying (coming from college or Atlanta or Los Angeles), but also where my grandparents were staying. Particularly as Papa got older, it just made more sense for people to come to us.

But that wasn't the case this year.

And maybe there's nothing to be read into that, but it seems to me that the "parents" in my family were no longer my own parents, but my brother and his wife. The "grandparents" that I knew so well were now great grandparents and, on my side of the family, at least, there was only one of those left. I was now less a son and more an uncle, although I'm sure my parents would take some umbrage to that statement. It seemed like my family had shifted. This had been going on for some time, but it never seemed so official.

And why not? This is the way that families and generations work.

Christmas Eve was relatively normal, aside from that. My brother and Wendy gave my grandma an "Angel of Remembrance" figurine in honor of Papa. Grandma began to shed a few tears, but aside from that the event didn't seem to be overly emotional, even though it was the first Christmas Eve without Papa. I think that perhaps the setting helped with that, as I could probably count on one hands the number of times I'd been at my brother's with my grandfather. It was pretty much like it was when I'm in Los Angeles: Papa was less gone and more somewhere else.

But that was Christmas Eve. Christmas would be a different story.

Late Christmas morning Nicole and I had brunch with my parents and my grandma. This was also the moment I would feel Papa's absence most directly, as opposed to an abstract sense that would come later. My parents have a formal dining area where we generally have all of our holiday meals. So, of course, we had brunch there, the five of us sitting around a dining room table that has been in my life as long as I can remember. Before we ate, my grandmother said grace.

This was something that could have happened any other year of my life. But this year there was no Papa. Generally speaking, Grandma said grace, even though Papa would be sitting at the head of the table. The fact that he didn't say grace was why he was able to give me the title for this book. But even though Grandma said the same words she's said over every meal we've ever shared at that table, Papa's presence was missing. He wasn't there to pat my hand and tell me how glad he was that I'd made the trip home. He'd laugh as he said that, a genuine laugh coming from a man who knew how important it was to have his family around him at such times. Then we'd start to eat and I'd watch as Papa mixed his food and ate in quick bites, a trait he picked up in the military.

Thinking about it now, I do find it somewhat strange that my grandma didn't mention Papa when she said grace. In years past she had been known to digress just a bit if something particularly important had happened recently. The first time I moved away she included me in grace. When the twins came home from the hospital she added something about them. When Connor made it home for Christmas Eve, she thanked God for his health. But she didn't mention Papa and I can only assume it's because it was still too soon for her. Only joyful things had made it into grace before, and while Papa's life was definitely something to be celebrated, we weren't done mourning yet.

Christmas afternoon was something of a circus, but in a good way. Over the years my family has managed to become a part of Wendy's family and as Wendy's own grandmother has gotten older and stopped hosting giant family holidays, two separate gatherings have merged into one big celebration.

Headcount: two great grandmothers, two grandmothers, one grand-father, one father, one mother, one uncle, one uncle's girlfriend, and two twin boys, age four. Of course, it's pretty easy to guess where most of our attention was. While I know it's important for me to see my parents and my brother, the truth is that I don't feel like I miss much when I go six months or so without seeing them. At the very least I'll exchange e-mails and/or phone calls within that span. But my nephews are at an age when six months is a lifetime. They are my first priority when I go home and the main reason I regret living so far away.

Needless to say, I spend a lot of time with them when I'm home, more so, I think, than anyone else, but I suppose that's to be expected.

This made me realize that, in years past, I've split my attention between them and my grandfather. I'm not saying that was a bad thing—far from it. But I don't think I ever realized just how much time I would devote to the extreme ends of my family. It seems like any time I didn't spend running around with Nathan and Connor, I spent sitting next to Papa. And a lot of times he and I wouldn't even have much to talk about, it was just a matter of being there. Papa didn't have to be an active participant; he just had to be there.

That's what was missing this Christmas; Papa's presence.

My grandma had only been in Kent for a week by this point, but I could tell that she was having difficulty finding her place in this new phase of her life. She had never been a regular fixture in the day to day life of either my parents or my brother, yet now she was. And my grandmother is so independent that it was clear to me that this was not a position she was comfortable with. So much of her life would now be tied up in others, to the point of challenging her own sense of solidarity. Without Papa there to root her, it felt like Grandma was adrift as to her role, and became just another person watching the twins run around the living room with their new Thomas the Train toys.

Papa's absence became even more noticeable when it was time for dinner. My parents' sink had backed up that morning and was completely non-functioning the entire day. My dad was trying to fix it, and just as dinner was ready he decided to take my brother and me to the basement to have another go.

With ten people (two of whom were four) for dinner, my mom had set up a second table, presumably for the twins and whoever was feeding them. Even if my brother, my dad, and I had been with everyone else to sit down to eat, there was no semblance of order. Because of this, there was no grace.

Had Papa been there, it would have been different. He would have sat at the head of the table and my mom would have sat me next to him. My dad would have left the pipes in the basement for later and Chris and Wendy would have made every effort to get the boys to sit still for thirty seconds. And my grandmother would have said grace and she would have thanked god for watching over my flight, for bringing me home, for bringing Nicole into the family, and for keeping all of us healthy for another year.

And everyone would have said "amen." And Papa would have patted my hand and we'd joke about the title of this book. And I'd tell him that I was close to finishing it and that I'd decided to wait until after Christmas to write the last chapter. And then I'd tell him that he was going to make both of us famous.

But none of that happened this year. None of it ever will.

Nicole and I left the next day, on our way back to Los Angeles, on my way back to finish this book.

19

Legacy

GIVEN HOW MUCH NICOLE AND I HAVE been through in our four and half years together, I suppose there was some level of justice in the fact that it was 78° and sunny on our wedding day. The weather was just one of the reasons we decided to get married in California. As a bonus, it was nice to tie the knot in the same state where my grandparents originally got married.

While my grandfather proposed through the mail, I did it in the rain, in the parking lot of an Irish bar. He had a ring, at least; I'd promised Nicole that we would pick out a ring together, after the fact. I did get to put that ring on her finger myself, though.

My grandmother used to tell me that I shouldn't wait too long to get married, because the longer I waited, the older she and Papa got, and the less likely it was that they'd be able to dance at my wedding. But Papa had been gone for nearly two years by the time I proposed and my grandmother is in no condition to do much of anything these days, let alone dance.

It would be crazy for me to compare my relationship with Nicole to Papa's relationship with my grandmother as equals, but that doesn't mean I can't hope that similarities do and will exist. It's doubtful that we'll ever have a 60th anniversary party. While my grandparents got married at the young ages of nineteen and twenty-one, Nicole and I got married at the relatively old ages of thirty and thirty-three. While they were barely in the same country before they married, Nicole and I lived together for most of our relationship. Our marriage was a natural progression of our life together, rather than a hasty decision made by the threat of continued war.

But Nicole and I love each other, we love being together, just as my grandparents did. And I have a feeling that, just like my grandparents, we'll be able to get through anything together.

At a certain point, I developed a default smile.

Nicole was still getting ready at her house, which wasn't too far from the hotel. My family and I were outside, getting our portraits done before the ceremony, a nice way to cut down on the number of pictures we'd have to get taken in the hour between ceremony and reception.

Nicole had arranged for pictures to be taken featuring dozens of different combinations of my family, which might have been exhausting if not for the fact that there weren't that many people to put into groups. It was just my brother, his wife, my dad, my mom, my cousin, and I. My nephews, a month shy of turning seven, were still a bit too rambunctious for a cross country journey. Leaving them at home with their other grandma also meant my brother and his wife could use this wedding as a much needed vacation. The only other member of my immediate family not at the wedding was my grandma.

The last three years have been hard for my grandmother. A woman who had once been so energized and forceful, who seemed nearly ageless, had become increasingly sad and listless, suddenly feeling her age in ways that no one expected. She told Megan that, on average, a widow dies just two years after her spouse. My cousin responded by telling my grandma that she wasn't average.

But I think my grandmother has lost the energy to be extraordinary. She'd left a life of over thirty-five years behind in Huber Heights, and she didn't have it in her to start over again. I think that the fact that my cousin lives with her when she's not at college is the only thing keeping her going, the only role she thinks she has to play. It would be easy for me to say that she's wrong, but I have no way of knowing what she's been through. I can't comprehend how difficult her life has become. I do know, though, that she's still very much needed, whether she knows it or not.

Grandma's reason for missing the wedding was that she was too old to handle traveling to California. I can't argue with that. But I also think that attending my wedding without Papa would have been like pouring salt into a wound that already won't heal. Papa would have been the center of attention at our wedding, not just because I had told so many people about him, but because of who he was—and no one would have been happier to see me finally walk down the aisle.

For my grandparents, it was "husbands and wives reunited in paradise." For Nicole and me, it's "husband and wife starting their life together in paradise."

There was some debate as to where we'd go for our honeymoon. Nicole and I had talked about our theoretical wedding and, by extension, our theoretical honeymoon, for years, and I'd always said I wanted to go to Australia. I've never done much traveling, so I figured that I should take full advantage of the opportunity. But it quickly became clear that the cost and the travel time would be prohibitive. There was also the fact that Nicole is a determined tourist who packs as much sight seeing into a trip as humanly possible (I actually sprained my knee during our trip to New York, just from all the walking). While fun, a trip to Australia would most likely be a once in a lifetime event, and thus crammed full of things to do each day. Going to Australia would be hectic, and not the relaxing destination we'd need after putting together and surviving a wedding.

As happens so often in my life, so often in this book, it was Nicole who came up with the perfect idea: we should go to Hawaii.

It's hard to wrap my brain around the fact that my mom lived in Hawaii for three years and has now spent the last forty years living in Ohio. That's not to say that Ohio doesn't have some very nice qualities, but it's practically night and day compared to Hawaii. I took Nicole and me a week to re-adjust to life back in the real world after we returned from Hawaii; I would imagine it takes my parents much longer, particularly since they usually return to an Ohio that has yet to break free of winter.

I suppose there's certain symmetry to our honeymoon in Hawaii compared to my grandparents' years there, as it seems to match with my relationship with Nicole as compared to their sixty-two years together. Our honeymoon could only provide me with the briefest glimpse of what their life might have been like, just as the few weeks of married life I've experienced so far can only give me a hint of what's to come. My grandparents lived an entire book together, while Nicole and I have only written the first few sentences.

I took *The Collected Short Stories of Ernest Hemingway* with me to Hawaii. While Hemingway was a generation older than Papa, I felt like his stories had some resonance to them. I could see my grandfather sharing the same views as Hemingway, sharing the same sense of exploration, the same joy of people and places.

Papa led a life of adventure. He traveled the world. But while Hawaii might have held a special place in his heart, his favorite place was with his family, side by side with Grandma, no matter where that might be.

I finally understand that. Hawaii was paradise, but it was only paradise because I was there with Nicole.

20

Symmetry

IN HIGH SCHOOL THEY TAUGHT ME that the final paragraph was supposed to summarize the main points of my paper. They also told me it was supposed to be five paragraphs long, so I suppose I'm somewhat beyond what my high school education taught me.

How do I end this? How do I summarize and conclude the story of my grandfather's life, or, more accurately, the story of me writing about his life? How do I close this book, this story that took him eighty-two years to live and has taken me years to write?

I won't lie; this has been a double-edged sword. When I started this book I mentioned that I was afraid that Papa would die because of it. I realize that's an irrational thing to think, but the fact remains that he did die during the course of my writing this. I'm sure there will always be a part of me that thinks I'm responsible for that, no matter how ridiculous that might sound.

I know, beyond a shadow of a doubt, that I've spent far too much time talking about myself, too much time talking about the present, and not enough time delving into the past. I started this book thinking that writing about *writing about* my grandfather would be an interesting narrative technique, something that would get people to pick up the book. I considered it to be the flash that would come before the substance, the snazzy one liner that would naturally lead to a deeper and more substantial core. It was never my intention for that story—the story of me—to overshadow Papa's story. In some ways I feel like it has, but at the same time I realize just how closely connected those two stories are.

Even more frightening than the thought that this is the end is the thought that this is just the beginning. I began this book as a way of giving exposure to a man who deserved it. I was going to tell the world about the things Papa had seen and done and they were going to be impressed by it. I was going to tell the tale of a man who had a singular view of history and who played a singular part in my life. This was going to be something he could tell his friends about, something we could share, aside from whiskey and water.

But now he's gone and I find myself in the position of trying to sell the story of his life after the fact. I'm no longer doing this simply as a way of recording his life; I'm not just attempting to get his life's story published. This is now a testament to who Papa was. What began as a historical retrospective tinged with personal involvement has became this incredibly emotional journey far beyond anything I could have predicted. It's gone from a rather biased history book to a tribute to an important person in my life that I should have known better.

I have to wonder if that's what this has become, then; less the story of my grandfather and more a cautionary tale for those who would take the older generations for granted. And if that's the case, would it really be a bad thing? Would it really be so bad if everyone who read this suddenly realized what they had, suddenly decided that maybe it was worth it to make that multi-hour drive, to place that phone call, to actually send that letter or e-mail? I don't know that I could complain if that's what people took away from this.

This is emotional for me. In some ways I'm almost scared to end this.

I'm scared because I don't know how. I don't know how to finish this in a way that will do him justice. In the end, I suppose it's simple.

This is for you, Papa. I hope I did you proud.

Acknowledgments

My thanks to Harley Patrick and Hellgate Press for taking a chance on an unknown book about an unknown man by an unknown writer.

Heartfelt gratitude to the Fork Tailed Devils, the Dolphins, the Sharks, and all those who answer the call to serve.

This book would not exist without the incredible generosity of Andrew William Sears, Jr. and Alan and Amy Vanderneut, two sides of my wonderful extended family.

Thank you to my immediate family, who let me air out their lives for the world to see, especially my grandmother, who allowed me to write about so much of her life.

My friends and family provided me with mental, emotional, and financial support more often than they thought they could or would, and always without question. I hope you all know how much I appreciate it.

None of this would have been possible without Nicole. For this and many other reasons, I will never be able to thank her enough.

Thank you.